ROBERTO BARTOLINI

W9-CQU-668

FLORENCE

and its hills

Edition of the "Practical Guide"
up to date according to the last rearrangements
of the Galleries and Museums

NOVA LVX

Publishing House Becocci - Florence

Tuscany is decorated with Florence like a ring with an expensive jewel; and such town is adorned with all sorts of good things, like a virginal neck of a beautiful necklace.

G. Dati, *La sfera*

PURPOSE AND USE OF THE NEW EDITION

Ever more aware of the usefulness of a truly practical guide that prevents unnecessary loss of time to the visitor, and taking advantage of my long experience as a tourist guide, I improved this new edition, bringing it up to date according to the recent reorganizations in the Galleries and Museums, and enriching in with new illustrations so that it may also remains as a small remembrance of the "city in the heart of everyone".
In order to make better use of this guide, I make the following suggestions:

1) **Read the brief useful notes at the beginning of the book regarding:** *the schedules of the Churches, Galleries, Museums etc.*

2) **Look over all the illustrations,** *divided into practical itineraries and special maps that allow one to easily choose the works that interest him most, and visit them according to the time and means at his disposal.*

3) **The double map of the city's monuments at the rear of the book** *(with numbers refering to the relative pages in the book) also serves to show how so many important monuments that are located near one another are not seen by a great majority of visitors, because of lack of organization which results in a great loss of time. In fact, most visitors enter to admire the famous Medici Chapels but few get to see the adjoining and no less important architectural complex of San Lorenzo by Brunelleschi, enriched by Michelangelo's celebrated Laurentian Library. The same holds true with the small but important Museo del Duomo (Cathedral Museum) located behind the Cathedral; with the Pazzi Chapel in the cloister of the church of Santa Croce; with the splendid Church of San Miniato, not far from Piazzale Michelangelo; with the celebrated frescos by Masaccio in the Church of the Carmine; and, another among so many outstanding examples, the Roman theatre located behind the Cathedral of Fiesole, which, although it is one of the most important testimonies of the history of that city, is ignored by most visitors.*
In the hope of rendering a better service to the reader, and overcoming the difficulties encountered in putting together a modest but nonetheless accurate work, I have tried to improve this new practical and illustrated guide of "our beautiful Florence", that I and my collegues have the responsability and honor of explaining.

ROBERTO BARTOLINI

Florence as it was

VISITING HOURS OF GALERIES AND MUSEUMS AND OTHER USEFUL INFORMATIONS
NATIONAL MUSEUMS

		VISITING HOURS		CLOSING DAY
		WEEK-DAY	SUNDAY	
GALLERIA DEGLI UFFIZI - loggiato degli Uffizi, 6	ticket L. 1.250	9-19,30	9-13	Monday
GALLERIA PALATINA - Palazzo Pitti, piazza Pitti	ticket L. 1.000	9-14	9-13	Monday
GALLERIA D'ARTE MODERNA Palazzo Pitti, piazza Pitti	ticket L. 1.000	9-14	9-13	Monday
APPARTAMENTI MONUMENTALI Palazzo Pitti, piazza Pitti	ticket L. 1.000	9-14	9-13	Monday
MUSEO DEGLI ARGENTI - Palazzo Pitti, piazza Pitti	ticket L. 1.000	9-14	9-13	Monday
MUSEO DELLE PORCELLANE Giardino di Boboli, piazza Pitti	ticket L. 1.000	9-14	9-13	Monday
COLLEZIONE CONTINI BONACOSSI Palazzo Pitti, piazza Pitti	ticket L. 750	9-14	9-13	Monday
GALLERIA ACCADEMIA - Via Ricasoli, 60	ticket L. 750	9-14	9-13	Monday
MUSEO DI S. MARCO - Piazza S. Marco, 1	ticket L. 750	9-14	9-13	Monday
MUSEO ARCHEOLOGICO - Via della Colonna, 36	ticket L. 750	9-14	9-13	Monday
CAPPELLE MEDICEE - Piazza Madonna	ticket L. 750	9-19	9-13	Monday
MUSEO NAZIONALE BARGELLO Via del Proconsolo, 4	ticket L. 750	9-14	9-13	Monday
MUSEO CASA FIORENTINA ANTICA Piazza Davanzati	ticket L. 750	9-14	9-13	Monday
OPIFICIO PIETRE DURE - Via Olfani, 78	ticket	9-13	—	Sunday
CENACOLO DEL GHIRLANDAIO Borgognissanti, 38	ticket	9-14	9-12	—

CITY MUSEUMS AND GALERIES
(Sunday free admittance)

		WEEK-DAY	SUNDAY	CLOSING DAY
PALAZZO VECCHIO E QUARTIERI MONUMENTALI - Piazza Signoria	ticket L. 500	9-19	8-13	Saturday
RACCOLTA DI ARTE MODERNA A. DELLA RAGIONE - Piazza Signoria	ticket L. 250	9-14	8-13	Thuesday
CHIOSTRI S. MARIA NOVELLA - Piazza S.M. Novella	ticket L. 500	9-14	8-13	Friday
FIRENZE COM'ERA E GIARDINO DELLE OBLATE Via Oriuolo, 4	ticket L. 500	9-14	8-13	Thursday
MUSEO BARDINI E GALLERIA CORSI - Piazza de' Mozzi	ticket L. 250	9-14	8-13	Wednesday
CENACOLO DI S. SPIRITO E FONDAZIONE ROMANO - Piazza S. Spirito	ticket L. 250	9-14	8-13	Monday

NATIONAL MUSEUMS

Are closed in the following days: 1st January, Eastern, April 25th, 1st of May, June 2nd, August 15th, Christmas.

THE CITY MUSEUMS are also closed the June 24th, the day of the patron St. John.

N THE NATIONAL MUSEUMS the admittance is free for the Italian citizens unter twenty and above sixty; for all the first and third Saturday and the second and fourth Sunday of the month.

The Editor will not consider himself responsible for the changes which might occur.

GENERAL INDEX

ITINERARIES

EXCURSIONS

MUSEUMS LESS FREQUENTED, THAT MERIT BEING VISITED

Principal Churches, Galleries, Museums and Palaces in alphabetical order

(for the page number see index pages 6-7)

Bell tower by Giotto

BRIDGES

Carraia
Grazie (alle)
Santa Trinita (di)
Vecchio
Verrazzano (da)
Vespucci

CHAPELS

Brancacci (Church of the Carmine)
Medici (S. Lorenzo)
Pazzi (S. Croce)
Princes (S. Lorenzo)
Spanish (S. Maria Novella)

CHURCHES

Badia
Baptistry
Carmine
Ognissanti
Orsanmichele
Parte Guelfa
San Carlo dei Lombardi
San Firenze
San Lorenzo
San Marco
San Miniato
San Salvatore
Santa Croce
San Martino
Santa Felicita
Santa Maria del Fiore (Cathedral)
S. Maria Novella
Santa Trinita
SS. Annunziata
SS. Apostoli
Santo Spirito

CLOISTERS

Degli Aranci (of the Oranges — Badia Fiorentina)
Dei Morti (SS. Annunziata)
San Lorenzo
Santa Croce
Sant'Antonino (St. Mark's)
Scalzo (dello) (Via Cavour, 69)
Verde (S. Maria Novella)

FRESCOES

Foligno (Via Faenza, 42)
Del Perugino (Via Colonna, 5)
S. Apollonia (Via XXVII Aprile, 5)
S. Salvi (Via S. Salvi, 16)

FORTRESSES

Basso (da)
Belvedere

GALLERIES

Accademy of Fine Arts (Via Ricasoli, 60)
Modern Art (Pitti Palace)
Palatine (Pitti Palace)
Royal Appartments (Pitti Palace)
Uffizi

GARDENS

Boboli

HOUSES

Of Dante (Via Dante Alighieri)
Of Michelangelo Buonarroti (Via Ghibellina, 10)

LIBRARIES

Laurentian (San Lorenzo)
National (Piazza Cavalleggeri)

8

LOGGIAS

Bigallo (del) (Piazza Duomo)
Innocenti (degli) SS. Annunziata
Mercato Nuovo (del)
Orcagna or della Signoria
or dei Lanzi
San Paolo (S. Maria Novella)

MUSEUMS

Anthropology and Ethnology
Archeological
Bandini (Fiesole)
Bardini
Conservatory of Luigi Cherubini
Dantesque (Dante's House)
Innocenti (degli)
Horne (Via dei Benci)
Medicean
National (Bargello)
Old Coaches (Pitti Palace)
Opera del Duomo
Opera di Santa Croce
Pietre Dure (Via Alfani, 80)
San Marco (Angelico)
Science
Silverware (Pitti Palace)
Stibbert (Via Montughi)
Topografical (Via S. Egidio)
Zoological "Specola"
(Via Romana)

OTHER PLACES OF INTEREST

Certosa (Monastery)
Convent of San Domenico
Convent of San Francesco
Fiesole
Orthodox church
San Domenico
Settignano
Stadium
Synagogue
Vincigliata

PALACES (Most important)

Antella
Arte della Lana
Bartolini-Salimbeni
Busini-Quaratesi
Canacci
Corsini
Davanzati
Gianfigliazzi
Gondi
Guadagni
Guicciardini
Medici-Riccardi
Parte Guelfa
Pitti
Podestà-Bargello
Ricasoli
Rosselli del Turco
Rucellai
Serristori
Spini-Feroni
Strozzi
Strozzino (dello)
Torrigiani
Uffizi (degli)
Vecchio (della Signoria)

PARKS

Cascine

SQUARES

Duomo
Libertà
Piazzale Michelangelo
Repubblica (della)
SS. Annunziata
S. Croce
S. Firenze
S. Lorenzo
S. Marco
S. Maria Novella
Signoria (della)
S. Spirito
S. Trinita

Fig. 1 - Signoria Square illuminated for the traditional soccer game in costume

HISTORICAL-ARTISTIC BACKGROUND

The origin of Florence goes back to the period of the Etruscan civilization. According to some historians, the Etruscans of Fiesole were the first to settle in the Arno valley. Later the Romans, after the war of Sulla, occupied this fertile location, and Ceasar's veterans founded, on the banks of the river, the colony with the auspicious name of "Florentia" (I cent. BC). St. Miniato, who brought Christianity to Florence, was here martyrized in the III century. During the barbaric invasions, Florence suffered the harsh sorts of the other Italian cities. In 1115, after having weakened the feudal Lords, the Florentine people formed a free Commune.

After nearby Fiesole was conquered (1125), a second circle of walls was built around Florence, since the first was now insufficient.

From the XII to the XVI centuries, Florence aesthetically acquires that physiogonomy that she still maintains, charactarized by the classical sense of proportion and the chromatic marble decoration.

In architecture, this first period is exemplified by the *Church of San Miniato* and the *Baptistry* while in sculpture, the *Pulpit* of *San Miniato* (1207) is the most notable example. In art, the great personalities of Cimabue and Giotto stand out and Dante becomes an important literary figure. At the end of the XIII cent. three important churches are erected: *Santa Maria Novella* for the Dominicans, *Santa Croce* for the Franciscans and the *Cathedral*, testimony to how Northern linearism is transformed in vast spaces with vigorously conceived monumental forms.

Together with religious architecture, civilian construction develops, the most notable examples being: the Palace of the Bargello, the *Palazzo Vecchio* and the *Loggia of the Signoria*, called of the *Lanzi*.

With Dante (1265-1321) and Giotto (1266-1337), Florence begins her glorious era in culture and art. In the school of *Arnolfo di Cambio* (1240-1302) and that of Giotto, Andrea Pisano da Pontedera (1295-1345), author of the first Baptistry gates, forms his style.

Cimabue (1240-1302) surpasses the Byzantine formulas still loitering in Florence. *Giotto*, his great pupil, frees Florentine art from all its ties with the past, introducing to art, especially painting, a new human language, rendered with profound and attentive observation. From Giotto derive *Taddeo Gaddi*, *Bernardo Daddi*, *Maso di Banco* and many others.

The great XIV century artists announce the coming of the XV century, glorious period of the "Renaissance" (rebirth) during which time Florence re-lives the illustrious era that Athens knew in ancient Greece.

Filippo Brunelleschi (1377-1446), architect, erects constructions based on a new conception of proportion and volume derived from classic art.

Donatello (1386-1466), friend and collaborator of Brunelleschi, freeing sculpture from all Gothic influences, creates his masterpieces, rich with profound humanity due to his attentive observation of nature.

Masaccio (1401-1428), despite his brief lifetime, inspired by Donatello and above all Brunelleschi, introduces new elements of perspective and color in his creations that make him the first "Renaissance" painter. His frescoes in the *Carmine Church*, monumentally figurative in their powerful humanity, open new and vaster horizons to Italian art.

Leon Battista Alberti (1404-1472), musician, painter and author of art treatises, is the theoretical head of Florentine architecture. *Michelozzo* (1396-1472) is the architect of the *Medici-Riccardi Palace*; *Benedetto da Maiano* of the *Strozzi Palace*; *Lorenzo Ghiberti* (1378-1455) goldsmith, architect and sculptor, enriches the Baptistry with his famous doors. Students and followers of Donatello continue more or less near to his style of art. Among these: *Bertoldo* (1420-1492), *Desiderio da Settignano* (1428-1464), *Mino da Fiesole* (1430-1484), and *Luca della Robbia* (1408-1482), Andrea, his nephew, and Giovanni, Andrea's son, who, with their terracotta works of art represent the most popular and wide spread figurative aspect of the Renaissance.

Inspired by Brunelleschi, Donatello and Masaccio are: *Andrea del Castagno* (1423-1457) who painted dramatic and realistic creations; *Paolo Uccello* (1397-1475), creator of perspective and volume; *Domenico Veneziano* who endows his work with natural light; *Filippo Lippi* who reconciles Masaccio's principles with Donatello's synthetic line. After the middle of the XV century, *Antonio del Pollaiolo* (1432-98) and *Botticelli* (1445-1510), artists of different temperaments, with their vibrant lines that generate volumes, elevate Florentine Renaissance art to higher levels.

At the end of the XV century, when the representatives of the first generation of Renaissance art have died out, *Leonardo* (1452-1519) and *Michelangelo* (1475-1564) appear on the horizon. The atmosphere of ultra-sensitive light and shadow that bathes the pictorial vision, called "sfumato", of the former, finds its correspondent in the dramatic and vehement "non-finito" (unfinished) of the latter, who leads architecture, sculpture and painting to the highest summits of the Renaissance.

With the fall of the Florentine Republic, Michelangelo, valiant defender of the city, leaves Florence profoundly embittered and goes to Rome where he dies. His body is brought back to Florence and buried in St. Croce. Also Leonardo, who had already left Florence and lived for a while in Milan, goes to France where he dies and is buried in Amboise.

In the 16th century Florence is still an active center of schools of art, the most important of which is that of the so-called "mannerists", creators of sensitive technical refinements. Among the most famous painters are: *Rosso Fiorentino*, *Pontormo* and *Bronzino*. In sculpture we remember *Giambologna* and *Cellini* (also a great gold-smith). In architecture: *Vasari*, *Ammannati* and *Buontalenti*.

In the XVII century Florentine art becomes provincial, even though artists such as *Giovanni da San Giovanni*, *Furini* and *Stefano della Bella* are worthy of consideration.

The XIX century, after a period of accademic controversies between classicists and romanticists, is punctualized by the artistic movement of the "Macchiaioli", among whom excel *Fattori* and *Signorini*. The splendid Tuscan country-side, the enchantment of the Arno, and the melody of the olive groves, are rendered chromatically by means of the "macchia" (spots of color), painting that can be considered, although on a provincial level, the Italian correspondent of the celebrated French Impressionism.

Reopening the brief historical background previously outlined up to 1125, despite the bloody fighting between the Guelphs and Ghibellines (the former backed by the Pope, the latter by the Emperor). Florence becomes wealthier because of the great expansion of her commerce, especially the wool and silk industries. In order to impede the export of secondary products the Tribunale di Mercanzia (Commercial Court) was created. No one could take part in the city government if he did not belong to one of the famous guilds. In order to partecipate in the government, Dante became a member of the Doctors and Apothacaries Guild.

With the crushing victory of the *Guelphs* over the *Ghibellines* (1267), the "Government of the Signori and Priori" is created. The struggles continue: the Guelphs split into *Bianchi* (whites) and *Neri* (blacks). Dante, who is a White, is exiled from the city, and, after having wandered around France and Italy, dies and is buried in Ravenna in 1321. Despite the furious internal fighting, the cities commerce continues to grow, even though the plague of 1348 decimates her population from 90,000 to 30,000 inhabitants.

Fig. 2 - St. Croce quarter during the flood of November 4, 1966.

GENEALOGICAL TREE OF THE MEDICI

GIOVANNI DI AVERARDO (Bicci) (1360-1429)
w. Piccarda di Od. Bueri

COSIMO the Elder
(1389-1464) « Pater Patriae »
w. Contessina dei Bardi

PIERO ''the Gou-   GIOVANNI   CARLO
ty'' (1416-69) w. Lu-   (d. 1463)   (d. 1492)
crezia Tornabuoni

LORENZO the Ma-   GIULIANO (killed in the
gnificent (1449-92)   Pazzi conspiracy, 1478)
w. Clarice Orsini
     GIULIO, Pope Clement
     VII from 1523 to 1534

PIERO II (1471-   GIOVANNI   GIULIANO Duke
1503) w. Alfonsi-   Pope Leo X   of Nemours
na Orsini   from 1513 to 1521   (1479-1516) w. Fi-
     liberta di Savoia

LORENZO (1492-1519) Duke of   IPPOLITO Cardi-
Urbino w. Maddalena de La Tour   nal (d. 1535)
d'Auvergne

ALESSANDRO (1510-1537) Duke   CATHERINE
(killed by Lorenzino) w. Marghe-   (1519-89) w. of
rita, daughter of Charles V. With   Henry II King of
him the branch of Cosimo the   France
Elder dies out

The Medici coat of arms originally contained
12 balls. This number was reduced under Lorenzo
the Magnificent and later brought down to 6 balls.
(1) From Cosimo I, the Medici, were Grand Dukes.

LORENZO (1395-1440)
w. Ginevra Cavalcanti

PIER FRANCESCO (d. 1467)
w. Laudomia Acciaiuoli
dei Duchi di Atene

LORENZO   GIOVANNI
(d. 1503)) Lord   (1467-1498)
of Piombino   w. Catherine Sforza

PIER FRANCESCO   LODOVICO (1498-
(d. 1457)   1526), called Gio-
w. Maria Soderini   vanni delle Bande
     Nere w. Maria
     Salviati

LORENZINO   COSIMO I (1519-
(1514-1547)   1574) (1) Duke and
Murderer of Duke   Grand Duke from
Alexander   1569 w. Eleonora
     of Toledo, 2.nd wi-
     fe Camilla Martelli

FRANCESCO I   FERDINANDO I
(1541-87) w. Gio-   (1549-1609) Car-
vanna of Austria   dinal, then Grand
2.nd wife Bian-   Duke; w. Christi-
ca Cappello   na of Lorraine

MARIA (1573-   COSIMO II
1643) wife of   (1590-1621) wife
Henry IV King   Maria Maddalena
of France   of Austria

FERDINANDO II   LEOPOLDO
(1610-70) w. Vitto-   (1617-1675),
ria della Rovere   Cardinal

COSIMO III (1642-1723) w.
Margherita Luigia of Orleans

GIAN GASTONE   ANNA MARIA
(1671-1737)   LUDOVICA
w. Anna Maria of   (1667-1743) w. of
Saxony   William, Palatine
     Elector. - Last of
     the Medici, she
     willed the trea-
     sures of art and
     of her ancestors
     to the city of
     Florence

HOUSE OF LORRAINE, SUCCESSORS TO THE MEDICI GRAND DUCHY

FRANCESCO STEFANO (1737), later took
the name of FRANCESCO II Emperor

LEOPOLDO I (1765-1790)   GIUSEPPE II
later Emperor   Emperor
     (d. 1790)
FERDINANDO III
(1791-1824)

LEOPOLDO II   For the Grand Dukes
(1824-1859)   of Lorraine, the da-
     tes in parentheses in-
     dicate the years of
     their rule.

The Lombard money lenders are succeeded by the great Florentine bankers under the patronage of St. Matthew. Because of their ability and honesty, they become so influential that Popes and Sovereigns turn to them for large loans, even choosing them as their treasurers.

The finalcial and banking center was the *Piazza of the Mercato Nuovo* (today called "straw market" or "Porcellino"), at that time without the portico. The financial transactions took place on 80 rug covered tables, on which were placed sacks full of gold "florins", the Florentine currency that was prized in all of Europe. Here, where the schedules of the port of Leghorn were also displayed, nobody who was armed was allowed to take part in the operations. Among the Florentine bankers, the Medici were the most powerful. Cosimo called "*the Elder*" (1389-1464), was the successor in the bank of his father Giovanni, gonfalonier of the city. The founder of a new banking system, he accumulates so much wealth, that he becomes the most influential man in the city government. He was hindered with every means by dangerous adversaries, among whom was Rinaldo degli Albizi who, unable to suppress him, had him exiled to Venice for ten years, where he further extends his financial empire. Because of his many influential acquaintances he shortens his exile, returns the following year acclaimed "Gentleman (Signore) of the city", and succeeds in driving his powerful enemies out of Florence. In order to avoid arousing jealousies Cosimo lives like a private citizen, however, placing the city in the hands of 70 faithful followers who govern for him. He is careful to protect the monastic orders who have such great influence on the people. Under his patronage, the Greek and Roman Churches meet at the Council of Florence (1439). Well known patron and prudent governor, he was honored with the title "Father of his Country". Cosimo's mediocre son *Piero*, called "the Gouty" who dies in 1469 of this illness, is succeeded by his grandson *Lorenzo.* He is no way hindered by his powerful adversaries who felt that, because he was so young, he would commit inevitable and irreparable errors that would automatically cause his removal from the government. But Lorenzo, having been prepared by his great mother Lucrezia Tornabuoni, governed Florence with such wisdom that he merited the title "Magnificent". From near and far his rivals prepared a conspiracy, headed by the Pazzi, which took place in the Cathedral on Easter morning 1478, where Lorenzo saves himself in the sacristy while Giuliano falls under the knives of the conspirators. Lorenzo, who now remains the only descendent of this great family, by avoiding any bloodshed to revenge his brother Giuliano, becomes even more popular. He wisely takes advantage of this sad situation to more easily get rid of his powerful enemies, thus becoming absolute heir, arbitrater of the city, and most prestigious man of the era. Heads of other Italian states turn to him for advice. Under Lorenzo, Florence lives the most glorious years of art and culture. Lorenzo's son Giovanni, young and brilliant Cardinal, becomes Pope Leo X (1513-21) and appoints many of his faithful followers to the office of Cardinal, thus preparing the Papacy for his cousin Cardinal Giulio (son of Giuliano assassinated in the Cathedral) who becomes Pope Clement VII (1523-32). Entering in the sphere of the Great European families, the Medici give two famous queens to France: *Catherine,* wife of Henry II and *Maria,* of Henry IV.

Upon the death of Lorenzo the Medici power seems to fall apart. Charles VIII of France enters Florence and Lorenzo's son Piero flees scorned by his countrymen. *Pier Capponi* becomes the arbitrator of the city and, threatening to "ring the bells" to call the people to arms to defend the city, he obligates the invading king to leave Florence (1494), which becomes a Republic once again.

Savonarola becomes head of the Republic. His ardent mission as a reformer places him against the powerful who, through intrigues, have him hanged and burned in Signoria Square with his followers Maruffi and Buonvicini (May 23, 1498).

The Medici return stronger than ever. The last dream of the Florentines to live in a free Republic vanishes after the memorable seige and heroic sacrifice of *Francesco Ferrucci* (1529) the champion of Florentine patriots. *Alexander Medici,* with the support of Charles V and Pope Clement VII (his relative), becomes the first Duke of the city. Revealing himself a tyrant, he is killed by his cousin *Lorenzino* (1537). With the slaying of Alexander ends the branch of Cosimo the Elder and the second branch of the Medici begins (as illustrated in the enclosed geneological tree of the Medici). *Cosimo I* (1519-1574), son of Giovanni delle Bande Nere (famous soldier) becomes absolute ruler of the city, and, from 1569, Grand Duke of Florence and Tuscany.

Cosimo I's successors soon become secondary figures in a vaster political and economic world. *Anna Maria Ludovica* (1667-1743), called "Electress Palatine", with the "Family Pact" drawn up in Vienna (1737), specifies that all the art treasures collected by her family are to remain in Florence to be forever enjoyed by the Florentines and the world. Thanks to this generous legacy, all the works of art taken during the last war were able to be recuperated.

After the Medici, Tuscany is ruled by the Dukes of Lorraine who are driven out in 1859. From 1865 to 1871 Florence was the capitol of the kingdom of Italy.

FIRST ITINERARY

Piazza della Signoria – Loggia della Signoria (dei Lanzi) – Palazzo Vecchio – Uffizi Gallery – Church of Orsanmichele – Via Calzaiuoli – Loggia del Bigallo – Piazza Duomo – Baptistry – Cathedral (Santa Maria del Fiore) – Bell Tower – Oratory of the Misericordia – Museum of the Opera del Duomo. (This itinerary is indicated by the numbers 10, 9, 2, 3 of the monumental map.)

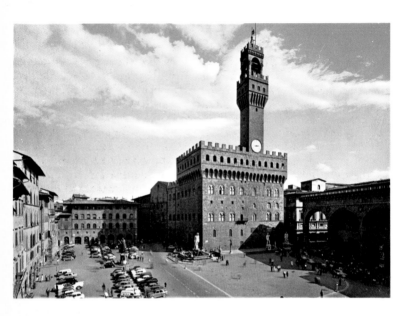

PIAZZA DELLA SIGNORIA (fig. 3)

Hearth of the origin and of the history of the Florentine Republic, the square still conserves its character as the political center of the city.

The square is dominated by the XIV century Palazzo Vecchio with the bold crenellated tower (fig. 3). On the right we can see the Uffizi Gallery and the Loggia della Signoria. On the left, at the end of the square: the Palace of the Tribunale della Mercanzia (Commercial Court) now the Bureau of Agriculture; to the left, at no. 7, the Uguccioni Palace, by Folfi (1549), with a bust of Cosimo I in the niche. In front of the Palazzo Vecchio is the Palace of the Assicurazioni Generali, by Landi (1871), whose much discussed imitation of the XV century architecture alters the characteristic basic unity of the Square. Beginning our look at the statues in the square, from left to right we observe: *the bronze equestrian statue of Cosimo I* by Giambologna (1594 – fig. 4) with *episodes of his reign* on the reliefs. Next follows the large *Fountain of Neptune* called "Biancone" by the Florentines (fig. 4) by Ammannati. The base of the fountain has interesting bronze figures of *nymphs and satyrs*, by collaborators of Ammannati, among whom was Giambologna. Near the center of the square a porphyry plaque commemorates the site where Savonarola and his followers Maruffi and Buonvicini were hanged and burned at the stake (5-23-1498). On the steps of the Palazzo Vecchio: *Lion* called "il Marzocco" (fig. 4) with the *Florentine Lily*, a copy of an original by Donatello in the National Museum.

On the granite pedestal, *Judith slayng Holofernes* (fig. 4) in bronze, a dramatic work of Donatello's maturity, that can be better admired from the top of the steps. Near the entrance of the Palace, copy of *David* that substitutes the original by Michelangelo, conserved in the Gallery of the Accademy of Fine Arts (Via Ricasoli 60). Followed by the heavy marble group of *Hercules and Cacus*, by Bandinelli (1533). At the entrance of the Palace the two statues at one time served to hold the chains that blocked the door. The female statue on the right is by Bandinelli while the male on the left by Vincenzo de' Rossi. Above the door of the Palace, the monogram between the two *Lions* reads: *Christ, King of the City.*

Loggia della Signoria. Called erroneously "dell'Orcagna" because at one time it was thought to be by this artist; called also dei Lanzi, because of the Swiss body-guards at the service of Cosimo who took cover here. Now we know that it was built by Benci di Cione and Simone Talenti (1376-82), for the investiture of the Priori and other celebrations of the Republic. It is a notable example of Florentine Gothic architecture, with the wide arches supported by solid pilasters that preludes to the Renaissance.

Above the arches are exquisite lobed panels with figures of the Virtues on a blue enamelled background carved from designs by Agnolo Gaddi. The splendid *Loggia* terminates on high with the vast panoramic terrace.

Under the Loggia: the famous Perseus holding the head of Medusa in bronze by Cellini (fig. 4). In the niches on the base are exquisite sculptures of *mythological figures* in which we see the artist's extraordinary ability as a sculpture and goldsmith together. The bas-relief, representing *Perseus freeing Andromeda*, is a copy of the one in the Bargello. (On the back of Perseus's head, the semblance of a human face can be detected. This is thought to be Cellini's self-portrait.)

Fig. 4 - Sculpture in Signoria Square: I) Menelaus supporting the body of Patroclus; II) Giambologna: Rape of the Sabine Women; III) Ammannati: Fountain of Neptune; IV) Lion called the "Marzocco„; V) Cellini: Perseus; VI) Donatello: Judith slaying Holoferness; VII) Giambologna: Hercules fighting the Centaur; Pio Fedi: Rape of Polixena.

On the steps of the Loggia are two statues of lions, the one on the right from the classical era and the one on the left is by Vacca (XVI cent.).

Under the right arch of the Loggia is the *Rape of the Sabine Women* (fig. 4), the famous marble group by Giambologna, with the same subject represented in bronze on the base.

In the second row the statues are from left to right; *the Rape of Polixena* by Pio Fedi (1886 – fig. 4); *Menelaus supporting the body of Patroclus* (fig. 4): *Hercules fighting the Centaur Nessus* (fig. 4).

Against the wall of the splendid Loggia are six restored antique statues, the third from the left of which is the most notable.

PALAZZO VECCHIO

The Palazzo Vecchio is attributed to Arnolfo di Cambio who began it in 1299, incorporating the ancient tower of the Foraboschi into its construction. After the death of Arnolfo in 1302, the palace was finished by other artists in 1314. The solid cubical shaped building is enriched by the thrust of the simple tower with its precious Lederle clock which terminates on high with the bell-tower surmounted by the cusp and the lively climbing lion.

In this public palace built as the seat of the Priori, later lived the Duke of Athens, who was driven out because of his tyranny. From 1540 to 1550 it was the home of Cosimo I who enlarged the construction. When Cosimo moved to the Pitti Palace this palace was identified with the name "vecchio" (old) to distinguish it from the new (Pitti) and this name remained. From Via Gondi the additions of the Palazzo Vecchio, executed in the XVI and XVII centuries, are clearly visible.

First Courtyard (fig. 5) remodelled in 1470 by Michelozzo. On high, around the courtyard are crests of the Church, City and the Guilds. In the center, the porphyry fountain with the lively winged boy, a copy of the original by Verrocchio now on the second floor. The columns, at one time smooth, were decorated with colored stucco designs in the XVI century. The frescoes on the walls, representing scenes of Austrian cities, were painted for the wedding of Francesco (son of Cosimo I) and Johanna of Austria. In the niche, *Samson and a Philistine* by Pierino da Vinci. In the corner on the left is the old *Armory*, conserved in its original style (generally closed).

Second Courtyard, observe the massive pillars built in 1494 to sustain the great *Salone dei Cinquecento* on the second floor.

Third Courtyard, is used for offices of the city. Between the first and second courtyards, the monumental stairs by Vasari leads to the

Salone dei Cinquecento (fig. 6). It was built in 1494 by Simone del Pollaiuolo, called "il Cronaca", on commission of Savonarola who, becoming spiritual leader of the Republic after the exile of the Medici, wanted it as the seat of the Grand Council consisting of 500 members. Later, under Cosimo I, the Hall was enlarged by Vasari. During this transformation famous works were lost including the cartoons of the "battle of Anghiari" by Leonardo and that of the "battle of Cascina" by Michelangelo, with which the two artists were supposed to decorate the walls of the room. Among the historic events which took place in this hall we remember the proclamation of the adherence of Tuscany to the Kingdom of Italy (1859). From 1865 to 1871, when Florence was the capital of Italy, the representatives held their meetings here. Now congresses, concerts and other public manifestations are held here. On the walls are enormous and pompous frescoes by Vasari and helpers (1550-1570), that represent, beginning with the wall opposite to the entrance, from left to right: 1) *The taking of Siena* (fig. 7); 2) *The Conquest of Porto Ercole*; 3) *Victory of Cosimo I at Marciano in Val di Chiana.* On the entrance wall, from left to right; 1) *Defeat of the Pisans at the Tower of S. Vincenzo*; 2) *Maximillian of Austria attempts the conquest of Leghorn*; 3) *Pisa attacked by the Florentine troops.* The ceiling is made up of 34 panels also by Vasari and followers representing *episodes from the life of Cosimo I*, culminating in the center with the *scene of his glorification as Grand Duke of Florence and Tuscany.*

On the north side of the Hall, illuminated by enormous windows, is the raised stage called the "Udienza", built by Cosimo I to receive citizens and ambassadors. Above are frescoes of historical episodes; among these, on the left, that of Boniface VIII receiving the ambassadors of foreign States and, seeing that they were all Florentines pronounces the famous words, "You Florentines are the quintessence". In the niches are sculptures by Bandinelli: in the center, that of *Leo X*; on the right *Charles V crowned by Clement VII.*

On the left, entrance to the vestibule that leads to the splendid "Salone dei Duecento", closed to the public because it is reserved for city functions.

Continuing in the Salone dei Cinquecento, along the walls we can admire valuable Medicean tapestries with *Stories of the life of St. John the Baptist*, taken from the frescoes by Andrea del Sarto. The statues that represent the *Labors of Hercules are* by Vincenzo de' Rossi, pupil of Bandinelli. In the niche at the south of the Hall

Fig. 5 - Palazzo Vecchio - Fountain of the first courtyard

Fig. 6 - Palazzo Vecchio - Salone dei Cinquecento (Hall of the Five Hundred)

is Michelangelo's famous *Victory* (fig. 8), destined for the tomb of Julius II, representing the triumph of virtue over vice. It was given the name Victory in 1921 when it was brought here from the Bargello Museum to celebrate the victory of World War I. In the lateral niches are antique sculptures.

On the right, through the glass door, we enter the *Small study-room (studiolo) of Francesco I Medici* (fig. 9), who was an expert in alchemy and had this small laboratory built for himself by Vasari (1570). It is a charming rectangular shaped room with a barrel vaulted ceiling frescoed by Poppi with *allegories of Prometheus and the Elements.* In the Lunettes are portraits of *Cosimo I and his wife Eleonor of Toledo* by Bronzino. Among the gracious sculptures is the *"Apollino"* by Giambologna. On the cabinet doors areinteresting paintings of the mysteries of alchemy and other mythological episodes, by Alessandro Allori, Cavalori, Macchietti and other artists of the late XVI century. Opening the door to the left at the back of the room, we climb to the secret archives from where we go down to the small treasure room reserved (it is believed) for the valuables of Cosimo I. Going back to the Studiolo, we return to the Salone dei Cinquecento. Through the glass door on the right of the opposite wall we climb to the "Hall of Leo X" (now the mayor's waiting

Fig. 7 - Salone dei Cinquecento - Vasari: Conquest of Siena
Fig. 8 - Salone dei Cinquecento - Michelangelo: Victory
Fig. 9 - Studiolo of Francesco I of the Medici

Quarters of the Priors (rooms 7-12)
later of Eleanor of Toledo
wife of Cosimo I

13. Chapel of the Signoria
14. Sala delle Udienze or Hall
    of Justice
15. Room of the Lilies
16. Old Chancellery
17. Guardaroba (wardrobe)
18. Study room

Appartments of the Elements

1. Room of the Elements
2. Terrace of Saturn
3. Hercules Room
4. Room of Jupiter
5. Room of Cybele
6. Ceres room

room) frescoed by Vasari with episodes from the life of this Medici
Pope. To the left of the fireplace is the Chapel that contains the copy
of Raphael's *Madonna dell'Impannata* (the original is in the Pitti
Palace). On the sides are frescoes of *SS. Cosmos and Damian,* patrons
of the Medici, in the semblance of Cosimo the Elder and Cosimo I.
On the right are other rooms of historical interest reserved for the
mayor's offices. In order to avoid the steep staircase that leads to
the third floor it is advisable to take the elevator which can be found
in the Salone.

Second Floor. Leaving the elevator, in the vestibule to the left (as
shown on the plan), after having observed the steep staircase with
the vault decorated with grotesques, we enter the rooms called the

Appartements of the Elements decorated by Vasari and helpers, representing on the walls in the First Room (fig. 10), *Allegories of
Water, Fire and Earth* and, on the ceiling, that of *Saturn.* Opening
the door in front we pass into the

Fig. 10 - Palazzo Vecchio - Sala degli Elementi (Appartment of the Elements)

Terrace of Saturn, so called because of the ceiling motif (recently restored), with its splendid Florentine roof. In the corner, the gracious little bronze devil by Giambologna (that one time decorated a corner of the Sassetti Palace). From here we can admire the façade of S. Croce; on the right of the Arno, Piazzale Michelangelo, S. Miniato, and, farther right the Fortress Belvedere. Looking down to the right, can be seen remains of the Church of S. Pietro Scheraggio incorporated into the Uffizi, and above, the passageway that joins the Uffizi to the Pitti Palace passing over the Ponte Vecchio. To the left is the Hercules Room that gets its name from the subject of the paintings on the ceiling. Also the tapestry has stories of Hercules. The room contains a *Madonna and Child* (Florentine school of the XVI cent.) and a valuable ebony cabinet (*stipo*) inlaid with semi-precious stones. From the vestibule (restored), we pass to the Room of Jupiter, named for the fresco of the ceiling On the walls are splendid *Florentine tapestries* made from cartoons by Stradano (XVI cent.). Returning to the Appartment of the Elements, on the left of the fireplace is the entrance to the

Room of Cybele. On the ceiling, the *Triumph of Cybele* and the *Four Seasons.* Against the walls, valuable cabinets (stipi) in tortoise shell and gilded bronze. The floor was made in 1556. From the

Fig. 11 - Palazzo Vecchio - Sala dell'Udienza (Audience Hall)

window observe the third courtyard of the Palace, bordered by the city government offices. Further ahead is the

Ceres Room, that gets its name from the motif on the ceiling work of Doceno, pupil of Vasari. On the walls are Florentine tapestries with hunting scenes, from cartoons by Stradano. Next is a study-room (that was the vestibule of an old hall) decorated by Vasari who represented *Calliope with Human and Divine Love*. Returning to the stair-case we come to the balcony, built by Cosimo I for the purpose of assisting, his family at the parties given in his honor in the Salone dei Cinquecento. Continuing through the corridor we enter the old Quarters of the Priori that Cosimo I had transformed into the *Appartments of his wife Eleanor of Toledo*. The first room is called

Sala Verde (Green Room because of the colors of the walls) with grotesque decorations on the ceiling by Ridolfo del Ghirlandaio. On the right is the Chapel frescoed by Bronzino (1564) with *stories of Moses*. By the same artist is the large *Pietà* on the altar. The small closed door on the left wall indicates the beginning of the passage-way that Cosimo I had Vasari build, leading to the Pitti Palace.

Room of the Sabines, from the ceiling decoration. At one time this

Fig. 12-13 - Palazzo Vecchio - Sala dei Gigli (portal) (Room of the Lilies) - Verrocchio: Winged Boy - Room 16, the former chencellery

was the room of the Ladies-in-waiting at the courth of Eleanor de Toledo. It contains *portraits of Medici Princes* by Sustermans, works of the Florentine school and a tapestry by Fevère (XVII cent.).

Dining-Room. On the ceiling, decorated by Stradano, is the *Coronation of Esther* with inscription in honor of Eleanor of Toledo. The room contains a XV cent. lavabo and two tapestries by Van Assel (1643) representing *Spring and Autumn*. From the windows observe the view of the courtyard and the first floor where Cosimo I had his appartments, separate from those of his wife, while above, to the right, were their children's appartments, now offices of the city.

Room of Penelope (room II on the plan). On the ceiling, *Penelope at the loom*; in the frieze, *episodes from the Odyssey*. On the walls: *Madonna and Child*, glazed terracotta and a *Madonna and Child with St. John*, in the manner of Botticelli.

Private Chamber of Eleanor called "Room of Gualdrada" from the subject of the ceiling, which Cosimo I had painted alluding to conjugal fidelity and representing the beautiful Gualdrada. daughter of Bellincione Berti degli Adimari, who refuses to kiss the Emperor Otto. Against the wall, a cabinet with Florentine mosaic designs. Farther ahead observe the Tower incorporated into the Palace. On

Fig. 14 - Palazzo Vecchio - Sala dei Gigli (Room of the Lilies)

the cabinet in the corridor is a *Mask of Dante*.

Chapel of the Signoria. Dedicated to St. Bernard and containing a *reliquary of the Saint*. The *Annunciation* is by Ridolfo del Ghirlandaio, who frescoed the walls (1514) imitating mosaic. On the altar is a painting representing the *Holy Family* by *Mariano da Pescia*. On the night between the 22-23 of May 1498, Savonarola and his followers spent their last hours in prayer in this chapel.

Following are some rooms, conserved in their original styles.

Sala delle Udienze o della Giustizia (fig. 11) (Hall of Justice). Here Savonarola was condemned to death together with his followers Maruffi and Buonvicini. Observe the beautiful carved ceiling, laminated with pure gold, by Benedetto da Maiano and Francione. On the portal of the Chapel, an *inscription in honor of Christ* (1529). The frescoes on the walls, of a highly decorative value representing *Stories of Camillus*, are by the brilliant mannerist artist Francesco Salviati (1550-60). Above the beautiful portal, statue of *Justice* by the brothers Giuliano and Benedetto da Maiano. The doors, intarsied with the figures of *Dante and Petrarch*, are by Giuliano da Maiano and Francione (1481).

Room of the Lilies (fig. 14). The magnificent *carved ceiling*, decorated with fleur-de-lys (that we also see on the walls), and the beautiful portal with the *Statue of St. John the Baptist and Putti* (fig. 12) are by Benedetto da Maiano and Francione. On the wall is the ample fresco (restored) by Domenico Ghirlandaio (1481-1485) who represented, from left to right, *Brutus, Muzio Scevola, St. Zanobius between SS. Lorenzo and Stephen, Scipione and Cicero*. From the window observe the splendid view of the city and the hills of Fiesole. Following on the left is the

Old Chancellery (recently restored). This was Macchiavelli's office when he was Secretary of the Republic. His bust in terracotta and his portrait are by Santi di Tito. In the center of the room, on the pedestal is the famous *Winged Boy* (fig. 13) by Verrocchio, brought here from the courtyard in 1959. Leaving here, on the left is the

Sala del Guardarobe (Wardrobe), where the Medici Grand Dukes kept their precious objects. The cupboards and carved ceiling are by Dionigi Nigetti (XVI cent.). On the doors of the cupboards, *53 maps of high scientific* interest, painted by Fra Ignazio Danti (1563) and Don Stefano Buonsignori (1575). In the center of the room the large *"mappa mundi"* ruined by excessive restorations.

In the back of the room, on the right, opening the door inserted between the cupboards, we pass to the terrace from where we can observe the old part of the Palace. Farther ahead,

The Study, richly decorated with grotesques. The room was used by Cellini to restore the treasures of the Medici princes. From the little window on the wall, Cosimo I spied his ministers at the meetings of the council held in the Salone dei Cinquecento.

Returning to the small terrace, observe on the left, the *stairs* that the Duke of Athens (driven out in 1343) had built for his security. From here we descend to other Monumental Quarters, conserved in their original style, where we can admire the art collection donated to the city of Florence by the American Charles Loeser (d. 1928). In the first rooms, are displayed the recuperated works of art that were stolen during the last war.

Heading toward the exit, returning to the Room of the Lillies, on the left we pass to the landing of the stairs that leads down to some rooms of historical interest, occupied by city officies. Above, the stairs leads to the gallery from where we can enjoy an ample panorama of the city and its hills. If possible, one can climb higher up to the little cell called the "Alberghettino" (little inn) where illustrious prisoners were held, including Cosimo the Elder, before his exile (1344) and Savonarola (1498).

Whoever climbs to the top of the Tower on a beautiful morning cannot forget the panoramic vision afforded from this historic Palace. From here the visitor can admire the city, recognizable in every monument, each of which is associated with a glorious name in history and art. To the north, the vast view of Fiesole and Settignano can be admired. To the south, Piazzale Michelangelo and San Miniato. We can see the Arno that flows slowly toward Pisa, flanked by the green Cascine Park. Farther away, the hills of Chianti. In the background are the Tuscan Apennines and the summits of Vallombrosa.

Upon request of the custodian found near the gallery, we can observe the function of the Lederle clock and the trap doors that open onto the square below into which, during the defense of the Palace, boiling oil and stones were dropped on the attackers. A bench dropped from here broke the left hand of Michelangelo's David, now restored.

Fig. 15 - View of the Uffizi and of Palazzo Vecchio

THE UFFIZI

Elegant manneristic building (fig. 15), that encloses between two wings the long and narrow Piazzale degli Uffizi, it was built for Cosimo I to house his administrative and judicial offices. It was begun by Giorgio Vasari (1559) and finished in 1585 by Bernardo Buonalenti and Alfonso Parigi. Closed on one side by the Lungarno, the building, with its closely spaced rhythmical and architraved portico, stretches out in ample openings and lengthens the scenery of Signoria square, joining the Palazzo Vecchio to the Arno. The Uffizi building, last of the post-Michelangelo creations, was inspired by the architecture of the Laurentian Library, although here, the plastic tension of Michelangelo becomes linear and decorative. The sculptures that we see in the niches of the pillars along the portico, representing famous Tuscans, are works of the last century. Among the most notable, that of St. Antonino by Giovanni Dupré (1854), and that of Niccolò Machiavelli by Lorenzo Bartolini (1846).

On the side of the building, facing Via della Ninna, and in the rooms on the ground floor of the Uffizi, can be seen important remains of the Romanesque church of *San Piero Scheraggio*, consecrated in 1608. When the building was constructed, the old church was incorporated into it. The church had been the seat of the community councils; here the popular reforms of Giano della Bella were promulgated (1292); and both Dante and Boccaccio made speeches to the public. The right wing of the Uffizi is preceded by the old Mint building, of which only the ground floor remains. Between this building and the beginning of the right wing of the portico, under the arch of Via Lambertesca, opens the Porta delle Suppliche (Door of the Supplications), original architecture of Bernardo Buontalenti, surmounted by a bust of Cosimo I attributed to Giovanni Bandini. Continuing along the Via Lambertesca, to the left can be seen the houses of the Pulci, today seat of the Georgofili, one of the oldest institutions for the study of the economic and agrarian sciences.

Actually in the Uffizi building are located the State Archives and the Uffizi Art Gallery. The State Archives, to which one accedes through one of the last doors of the left loggia, contains the collection of documents relating to the history of Florence and Tuscany, from their beginning up to modern times. Besides the collections and the specialized library, there is also an interesting exposition room in which documents and curios of the history of Florence and Italy placed in glass showcases, can be seen. Among the most famous documents ore the Fiorinaio, or register of the Florentine Mint; the charter of union between the Greek and Latin churches (1439); the book of the Chiodo, containing the condemnation of Dante, and considerable nautical maps. In order to avert the danger of fires and to allow the Uffizi Gallery to use these vast rooms for displaying the many works of art not visible to the public because of lack of space the State Archives will soon be moved elsewhere.

Under the portico, near the Palazzo Vecchio, between the 19th century statues of *Lorenzo the Magnificent* and *Cosimo the Elder*, is the entrance to the Gallery.

THE UFFIZI GALLERY
(located on the III floor)

The project to arrange the Gallery on the 3rd floor of this large building, conceived by Cosimo I Medici, was realized by his son Francesco I, who, after having Buontalenti build the room of the Tribune for the collection of antique medals and other works of art had the cielings of the first corridor decorated so that he could place the series of famous portraits and, above all, the valuable sculptures that give it the name of « Gallery of the Sculptures ». With the addition of the other rooms, the Gallery was enlarged with the work brought from Rome by Ferdinand I, who renounced the office of Cardinal to become Grand Duke of Tuscany in the place of his deceased brother Francesco I. The Medici (see enclosed genealogical tree) now absolute rulers of the city and of Tuscany, having married into the greatest families, continuously enriched the Gallery, as under the reign of Ferdinando II, who married Vittoria della Rovere. Later Cosimo III had the Gallery made larger in order to house the work inherited from his uncle Cardinal Leopold. With the extinction of the Medici, the last of the family, Anna Maria Ludovica, who died in 1737, with the so called « family-pact » held in Vienna in 1737, arranged that all the art treasures gathered by the powerful dynasty forever remain at the disposal of the Florentines and of the visitor of the entire world. Thanks to this testament, it was possible to recuperate so many works of art stolen during the last war, and during the Napoleonic era, even though, unfortunately, many masterpieces remained in France.

The Lorraines, successors of the Medici, enriched the Gallery and

PLAN OF THE UFFIZI GALLERY

A - Vestibule of the gallery
B - Passage to the Signoria palace
C - Uffizi
D - First corridor
E - Second corridor
F - Third corridor
G - Staircase to the corridor of Vasari and to the collection of the self-portraits
H - Belvedere
I - Bar
L - New staircases 43, 44, 45
L - New little halls 43

1. Hermaphrodite's hall (old sculpture)
2. Hall of the '200
3. Hall of the Siennese painting of the '300
4. Hall of the Florentine painting of the '300
5.6. Hall of the gothic painting
7. Hall of the first Renaissance
8. Hall of Lippi, Pollaiolo, Angelico
9. Hall of Pollaiolo and Botticelli
10. Botticelli's hall
10. Botticelli's little hall
12. Flemings' little hall
13. Filippino Lippi's little hall
14. Van der Goes's hall
15. Hall of Leonardo and Verrocchio
16. Hall of the geographical maps
17. Little hall of the Umbrian painting school
18. Hall of the tribune
19. Hall of Perugino and Francia
20. Hall of Mantegna and Dürer
21. Hall of Bellini and Giorgione
22. Hall of Holbein and Altdorfer
23. Correggio's hall
24. Hall of the miniatures
25. Little hall of the Emilian painting school
26. Andrea del Sarto's hall
27. Pontorno's hall
28. Tiziano's hall
29. Parmigianino's hall
30. Hall of Raffaello and Michelangelo
31. Dosso-Dossi's hall
32. Sebastiano del Piombo's hall
33. Corridor of the '500
34. Veronese's hall
35. Hall of Tintoretto and Baroccio
36-40. Vestibolo della Scala di Buontalenti V.L.
41. Ruben's hall
42. Niobe's hall

Fig. 16 - First Corridor of the Gallery

built the beautiful room of the Niobe to house the marble group
called Niobe and her children struck by Apollo and Diana. After
the expulsion of the Lorraine (1859), the Gallery passed under
the State and was completely reorganized according to modern
criteria. With the reorganization that took place after the last war,
not only can we more clearly admire the development of Florentine
and Tuscan painting and the great influence that it exercised over the
other regions, but also we can better observe the great benefits that
both Italian and foreign artists obtained by coming into contact
with each other, as illustrated by the *Adoration of the Shepherds*
by Van der Goes in Room 14, placed in controntation with works
by Florentine artists who were inspired by this painting. Thus the
works of Bellini confronted with those of Dürer, clearly show the
fascination that the great German artist experienced on contact with
the Venetian painters.

First Vestibule with the ticket counter, where temporarily an antique
copy of the marble group of *Mars and Venus* has been placed. O
recent date is the resystematization of the presbytery and the abs
of San Piero Scheraggio, that holds frescoes detached from variou
Florentine churches and placed here momentarily.

Figs. 17-18 - Giotto and Cimabue: Madonna Enthroned with Angels

Second Vestibule. On the left wall dominates the large portrait of the Flemish school representing *Anna Maria Ludovica de' Medici.* On the right wall, columns of the old church of San Piero Scheraggio, on which remains of 13th century frescoes can be detected. On the left begins the monumental staircase by Vasari, decorated with ancient Roman busts.

On the first floor is located the famous collection of *Drawings and Prints* begun by Cardinal Leopold de' Medici, reserved for scholars. In the first room periodically are held expositions of graphics and drawings by foreign and Italian artists, to which there is no charge for entrance.

In order to avoid the 126 step climb of the staircase, it is advisable to use the lift that takes you to the top floor. Before entering the Gallery, one can admire Vasari's splendid staircase from above. Past the ticket control is the vestibule decorated with panoplies and trophies of late Roman art.

First corridor of the Gallery (fig. 16). From the windows observe the architectonic complex of the buildings, erected by the Medici to house their administrative offices on the first floor. The long loggia that originally topped the building was closed with wide windows.

Fig. 19 - Simone Martini: Annunciation

The frescoes on the ceiling in this first corridor, with mythological and grotesque motives, were painted by the Florentine artists Bizzelli, Butteri, Pieroni and Alessandro Allori in 1581, inspired by the Vatican Loggia. Badly damaged on the night of August 4, 1944, when the Germans blew up the bridges over the Arno, these valuable frescoes, that because of so many catastrophies seemed irreparably lost, were able to be restored after four years of patient and able restoration. On the wall of the long corridor can be admired valuable tapestries in the following order: in the first, *Wolf and Wild Boar Hunting*, work of Squilli, following cartoons by Stradano. Ahead we can admire the *months of the year*, with bizarre grotesque scenes on yellow backgrounds, work of the Flemmish tapestry makers Karcher and Roost following cartoons by the imaginative painter Bachiacca (1549-53). These two craftsmen began the famous Medici Tapestry Manufacture. Then follows the rich series of Belgian tapestries representing scenes of *Festivities and Tournaments at the Court of Catherine de' Medici and Henry III*, the cartoons of which are attributed to François Quesnell (1575-80).

The visit to the Gallery begins in

Room 2, *dedicated to Cimabue and Giotto*. In direct confrontation Giotto and Cimabue: Madonnas Enthroned with Angels and other artists of the same period. On the right wall we see the famous *Madonna enthroned with Angels* by Cimabue (fig. 18), originally in the church of St. Trinità, dated around 1275. A work greatly nourished by the Byzantine culture, especially in the soft colors, in the gold touches of the Madonna's dress and in the details of the drawing, obtained in the perspective of the throne and the degrading of the angels that reveals, with the beginning of a new style, the foundations of the future evolution of Florentine art.

On the left wall, opposite to Cimabue, the famous *Madonna and Child with Angels* formerly in the Rucellai Chapel in Santa Maria Novella, for centuries believed to be by Cimabue, is attributed to Duccio di Buoninsegna, although authoritative critics still believe it to be the work of a master between Cimabue and Duccio, known as the « Master of the Rucellai Madonna ». The solemnity of the painting, with its traditionally Byzantine colors, with the majestic figure of the Madonna and the Prophets and Saints in the beautiful frame rendered with a miniaturist's delicacy, contribute to assigning this work to Duccio.

In front of the entrance dominates the famous, grandiose *Madonna*

Fig. 20 - Gentile da Fabriano: Adoration of the Magi
Fig. 21 - Paolo Uccello: Battle of San Romano

Enthroned with Angels and Saints by Giotto (fig. 17), originally in the church of Ognissanti. One of the most solemn creations of this great innovator of Florentine and Italian art, chronologically placed between the frescoes of Assisi and those in the Scrovegni Chapel in Padua (1303-05). In this work Giotto discloses all his powerful personality as far as space and form are concerned. While the color contributes for the first time in illuminating the figures, rendered profoundly human, the soft chiaroscuro helps to make this great work compact, volumetric and monumental.

Also by Giotto is the *Polyptych* displayed on the stand to the left, that came from the Church of the Badia.

On the wall beginning left of the entrance are: *Madonna and Child* (Florentine school, c. 1270); *Crucifix and Stories of the Passion* (Lucchese school, middle of the 13th cent.); *St. Luke* by the « Master of the Maddalena ». On the right wall from the entrance are: the *Stigmata of St. Francis and Christ Crucified*, in the manner of Bonaventura Berlinghieri; the *Savior between the Virgin and SS. Peter, John and Paul* by Meliore Toscano (c. 1271). On the following wall, *Crucifix and Stories of the Passion*, Pisan school of the middle of the 12th century.

Then follows

Room 3, *dedicated to 14th century Sienese painting*. Beginning on the left, *Stories of the Life of the Beata Umiltà*, originally in the church of the Donne di Faenza; followed by a *Nativity* by the Bolognese painter Simone de' Crocifissi, and a *Presentation in the Temple* by the Sienese Bonaccorsi. Then the famous *Annunciation* by Simone Martini (1333), originally in the Cathedral of Siena, one of the most important creations by this leader of the Sienese school, rendered with musical rhythm and a miniaturistic quality (fig. 19). On the sides observe the figures of *SS. Ansanus and Giulitta* by Lippo Memmi, pupil and brother-in-law of Simone, who attempts to emulate the fluidity of the line and delicate form of the master. The room also contains the *Madonna and Child* by the Sienese Niccolò di Ser Sozzo Tegliacci (the date can be read 1315 or 1341), and, the *Four Stories of the Life of St. Nicola di Bari* and the delicate *Presentation in the Temple* (the latter dated 1342) by Ambrogio Lorenzetti, brother of Piero, and with him considered one of the most important Sienese artists of the 14th century.

Room 4. *Dedicated to 14th century Florentine and Lombard painting.* On the long left wall are shown fragments of a polyptych with *Saints, Martyrs and Virgins*, by the Lombard Giovanni da Milano, of northern formation, which he reveals in the soft chiaroscuro rendered with acute realism, but at the same time, aware of the art of Giot-

Fig. 22 - Masaccio: St. Anne Enthroned with the Madonna and Child
Fig. 23 - Piero della Francesca: Portrait of Battista Sforza
Fig. 24 - Piero della Francesca: Portrait of Federico da Montefeltro

to. This is followed by the grandiose painting by Andrea Orcagna, representing St. Matthew. On the following wall, *Madonna and Saints*, polyptych by Bernardo Daddi. On the right wall, *Deposition*, attributed to Giottino, once thought to be by Maso di Banco, very close (perhaps the greatest) follower of Giotto. Giottino is one of the most remarkable Florentine painters of the 14th century, sensitive to northern color and to soft chiaroscuro. Next, *Madonna and Child with Angels* by the Florentine artist Taddeo Gaddi, one of the most faithful followers of Giotto. Also shown are works by Nardo di Cione, Bernardo Daddi, Jacopo del Casentino and others.

Rooms 5-6. *Dedicated to works by artists of the so called « International Gothic » that fluorished between the end of the 14th century and the beginning of the 15th century.* From left entering, the famous *Adoration of the Magi*, by Lorenzo Monaco, teacher of Beato Angelico (circa 1420), bright and fantastic work by this Sienese artist who was active in Florence and became one of the major late Gothic painters.

On the wall in front is the *Adoration of the Magi* by Gentile da Fabriano (fig. 20), formerly in the church of St. Trinità. Gentile is a late Gothic artist, fantastic and courtly in appearance, while his deep color and plastic values are already Renaissance. On the following wall, by the same artist: *Four Saints*, fragment of a work once in the Quaratesi Chapel in San Niccolò, dated about 1424. Next the large *Incoronation of the Virgin* by Lorenzo Monaco (1413). On the small back wall, the graceful and imaginative *Tebaide*, representing the life of the hermits in the desert, believed by some critics to be by Gherardo Starnina, and by others, by the hand of Beato Angelico, during the period when Masaccio's influence was greatly felt.

Room 7. *Dedicated to early Renaissance.* On the left wall the famous *Battle of San Romano* by Paolo Uccello (1456) (fig. 21). It is the central part of a series of paintings, one of which is in the Louvre, and the other in the National Gallery of London. The artist, in his tense perspective study, here faces the typical Renaissance problems of foreshortenings, crystallizing figures, landscapes, horses, armor and arms in immobile volumes.

On the easel, the famous *Portraits of Federico da Montefeltro Duke of Urbino and his Wife Battista Sforza* (figs. 23-24) by Piero della Francesca (1456-66). On the back, the *Triumphs of the Duke and Duchess*. He represents the subjects on marble terraces against a midday sun that hits the distant landscape. A creation rendered with an

Fig. 25 - Beato Angelico: Incoronation of the Virgin

extremely poetic geometric abstraction, exalted in the fullness of the light, against a vast landscape. Here the Flemish suggestions are surpassed in a completely new synthetic vision. With the inheritance of Vittoria della Rovere, wife of Ferdinand II Medici, the work passed over to the Uffizi in 1631, together with other art treasures.

On the opposite wall, *St. Anne Enthroned with the Madonna and Child* (fig. 22), work done in collaboration by Masolino and Masaccio, who shows a style already full and mature, despite his young age. On the right, *Madonna Enthroned with Saints* (c. 1445), by Domenico Veneziano, formerly in the church of St. Lucia de' Magnoli, a work which vibrates in the color rendered luminous by the day light that covers the spaces and palpitates in the figures painted with intense humanity. On the next wall, *Madonna and Child*, by Beato Angelico, and a valuable predella by Filippo Lippi representing *St. Frediano deviating the Serchio*; *Announcement of the death of the Virgin* and *St. Augustine in his study*. These two artists are best represented in the following room where Lippi's major works are displayed.

Room 8. *Dedicated to Filippo Lippi, to the brothers Antonio and Piero del Pollaiuolo and other 15th century artists.* Here we can admire the famous *Madonna and Child with Two Angels* (fig. 26) by Filippo Lippi, whose art was formed under the influence of Masaccio, especially in the plastic construction of the figures. On the small left wall, *SS. Vincent, James and Eustace*, originally in the basilica of San Miniato, by Antonio and Piero Pollaiuolo, with the prevalence of Antonio, the greater of the two. On the left wall, *Incoronation of the Virgin* by Beato Angelico (fig. 25), a delicate painter, who translates Medieval mysticism into his delicate Renaissance lyricism. On the far wall, large *Incoronation of the Virgin*, early work of Filippo Lippi. On the lower left wall, predella of altar-piece (formerly in St. Croce) showing the *Pietà, The Mystic Marriage of St. Catherine* and *Two Saints*, by Benozzo Gozzoli, pupil of Angelico. Finally, on the next wall, to the left, *Madonna and Child* and *Annunciation* by Alessio Baldovinetti, pupil of Domenico Veneziano, more sensitive toward linearity than light values.

Room 9. *Dedicated to the Pollaiuolo brothers and to the young works of Sandro Filipepi, called Botticelli.* On entering to the right, *Three Virtues* by Piero del Pollaiuolo: on the back of the first one observe the vigorous sketch of *Charity*, by his brother Antonio, great gold smith and sculptor of the second half of the 15th century. By Antonio are the other three *Virtues* on the next wall, beside the *Fortitude* by Botticelli, executed for the stalls of the Merchant's Tribunal. Comparing these works permits us to observe how these two artists, with their common vibrating lines, arrived at different results. On the easel we can admire Botticelli's small *Judith with her Handmaid Carrying the Head of Holofernes* and, on the back, *Holofernes Slain in his Tent*. On the wall, together with other young works of Botticelli, is the *Portrait of an Unknown Man holding a Medal of Cosimo the Elder*, perhaps portraying Piero de' Medici (fig. 27). Next *Portrait of a Noble Lady*, by Antonio del Pollaiuolo (fig. 28).

Room 10. *Entirely dedicated to Botticelli.* Between the melancholy

Fig. 26 - Filippo Lippi: Madonna and Child with two Angels

Fig. 27 - Botticelli: Portrait of an Unknown Man
Fig. 28 - A. Pollaiolo: Portrait of a Noble Lady
Fig. 29 - Botticelli: Allegory of Springtime

Figs. 30-31 - Botticelli: Allegory of the Birth of Venus and Calumny

49

Madonna of the Pomagranate and the brighter and musical *Madonna of the Magnificat*, of the artist's maturity (1478), typical representation of humanistic Florence at the time of Lorenzo the Magnificent and Politian, can be admired the celebrated *Allegory of Springtime* (fig. 29). The lyrical scene that takes place in the fresh green forest is dominated by the bright figure of Venus. On the right are the figures of Springtime who is strewing flowers and Flora being chased by Zephyr. On the left, the famous three Graces dancing, clothed in their transparent veils, being shot at with arrows by a blindfolded Cupid, and the figure of Mercury, who is clearing away the last of the morning's mist. On the following wall is the *Birth of Venus* (fig. 30) that the artist painted on canvas (c. 1486), idealizing the beautiful and fragile Simonetta, loved by Giuliano, brother of Lorenzo the Magnificent. It is a rhythmic creation with soft colors rendered in tones as cool as a marine dawn, also inspired by the verses of Politian. On the next wall, beside the *Madonna and Child with Saints*, observe the rhythmic *Annunciation* with its beautiful Florentine landscape (c. 1490). To the right of the opening is the *Adoration of the Magi* (1475), where, among the personages we see three generations of Medici portrayed: Cosimo the Elder, above; below his sons Piero and Giovanni; to the left Lorenzo the Magnificent, leaning on his sword (power) on the right, the dark haired Giuliano, who loved the beautiful Simonetta. The figure on the right with the yellow robe is thought to be a self-portrait of Botticelli. This painting is followed by Botticelli's *Pallas and the Centaur*, and finally, the *Madonna of St. Barnabas*, formerly in the church of the same name.

Room 11. *Botticelli.* Contains smaller paintings among which are: *St. Augustine in his cell*; and *St. Augustine and a child on the Seashore*. To the left, the famous *Allegory of Calumny*, that Botticelli supposedly painted while incited by the sermons of Fra Savonarola. The scene is represented under the static architecture of a beautiful classical portico, with, in the background a calm sea under a serene sky. The closeknit group of figures vigorously animates the scene (fig. 31), in which even the statues in the niches seem to participate. In this drama alluding to human injustice, we can see King Midas, with donkey's ears who, seated on his throne, listens to his poor advisers, Ignorance and Suspician. The hooded figures is Calumny, who raises his arm toward the foolish king in order to add more solemnity to what he is about to say. Envy, Deceipt and Malice are

Fig. 32 - Filippino Lippi: Self-portrait

Fig. 33 - Van der Goes: Adoration of the Shepherds

Fig. 34 - Lorenzo di Credi: Annunciation

the three women who drag the innocent victim before the King. On the left, Remorse clothed in black, looking back at the nude Truth who serenly turns her glance toward heaven. On the far wall, *Adoration of the Child and St. Jerome*, by Botticelli's major pupil Filippino Lippi, son of Filippo Lippi.

Room 12. *Dedicated to the Flemish artists*, who gave to Italian art their naturalistic and luministic qualities, as evident in the *Deposition* by Roger Van der Weyden, painted – it is believed – during his sojourn in Italy. Of his follower Hans Memling are displayed works of acute realism, as can be seen in some portraits and the *Madonna and Two Angels*. Following on the left.

Room 13. *Dedicated to Filippino Lippi and Lorenzo di Credi*, whose *Venus* is shown. Flanking this, a delicate *self-portrait* of Filippino Lippi (fig. 32) and the engraved portrait of an *Old Florentine*, by the same artist.

Room 14. *Dedicated to the large Portinari Triptych* by Van der Goes. It was painted in Bruges (1476-78) for Tommaso Portinari, director of the Medici bank in that city. In the central section, *Adoration of the Shepherds* (fig. 33); on the left leafs, *SS. Anthony and Thomas*

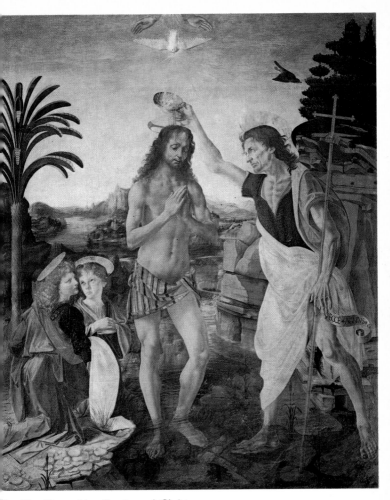

Fig. 35 - Verrocchio: Baptism of Christ

with the commissioner and his two sons; on the right leaf, *SS. Margaret and Mary Magdalen with Maria Portinari and her daughter.* This work was deservedly famous because of its acute and poetic human observation of the figures and of nature, rendered with subtle and complex shading of color. On the back of the leaves that were closed to protect the central section are splendid chiaroscuro figures representing the *Annunciation*. For confrontation purposes, on the surrounding walls are displayed works of Lorenzo di Credi, Ghir-

Fig. 36 - Leonardo: Adoration of the Magi

landaio and Filippino Lippi, who were influenced by the Flemish
painter. On the opposite wall is the *Resurrection of Lazarus*, by
Nicholas Froment from Avignon, also inspired by Van der Goes, who
obtained scenes of acute realism even in the outer leaves of the triptych.

Room 15. *Verrocchio, Signorelli, Leonardo and others of their group.*
Entering on the left, is the *Annunciation* (fig. 34) by Lorenzo di
Credi, sensitive to the influence of his fellow apprentice Leonardo.
The painting, of modest proportions, is the most valuable of the
artist, who, in the school of Verrocchio, surpassed the pictorial qua-
lity of the master. On the right, *Holy Family* by Luca Signorelli of

Cortona, one of the most interesting artists of the second half of the 15th century. Sensitive to Piero della Francesca's teachings about space, he was inspired by Leonardo's shading and Pollaiuolo's design, giving volume and movement to his creations. Next to the door, the famous painting of the *Baptism of Christ* (fig. 35), that Verrocchio, more well known as a sculptor than as a painter, began in 1470 with the help of the young Leonardo, whose hand is recognized in the angel on the left shown in profile. A simple and luminous painting, with a suggestively beautiful landscape. On the right, *Deposition* by Perugino, work belonging to the Florentine period of this Umbrian painter, who was Raphael's teacher.

The central wall is dominated by the celebrated *Adoration of the*

Fig. 37 - Leonardo: Annunciation

Magi by Leonardo da Vinci (fig. 36), painted for the brothers of the church of San Donato Scopeto, left incomplete by the great artist and scientist who was called to Milan by Ludovico il Moro. Despite the fact that the painting is left in its preparatory state, we can see the importance of Leonardo's invention of « sfumato » (shading), that was so widely diffused in the successive Lombard and Tuscan schools of painting. Also notice the solemnity of the scene, shown in a pyramid composition, the majesty of the architectonic and landscape elements, and the extraordinary variety of human types and expressions. This work reveals Leonardo's personality in full, his continuous and tireless research and attention to nature and humanity in all its aspects.

Room 16. *Called of the Maps*, because maps of Tuscany were painted

Fig. 38 - Pontormo: Portrait of Cosimo the Elder
Fig. 39 - Vasari: Lorenzo the Magnificent
Fig. 40 - Bronzino: Portrait of Lucrezia Panciatichi
Fig. 41 - Bronzino: Portrait of Prince Mediceo don Garcia

Fig. 42 - Bronzino: Portrait of Princess Medicea Isabella
Fig. 43 - Perugino: Portrait of Young Man
Fig. 44 - Mantegna: Triptych of the "Madonna of the Caves"

on the walls by Stefano Buonsignori (1589). On the ceiling are scenes of *mythological and allegorical subjects* by Jacopo Zucchi. This room contains the famous and much discussed *Annunciation* (fig. 37), with the luminous and idealized Tuscan landscape, that Leonardo painted while in Verrocchio's workshop. From the windows of the room can be seen a panorama of the east side of the city, from the church of S. Croce to the hills of San Miniato and Belvedere.

We return to Room 15 and, continuing along the corridor, we arrive at Room 18, the Tribune. From here, through a small door on the left we enter:

Room 17. Where, after the recent restorations, the statue of the *Hermaphrodite*, (formerly in room 1), has been placed. According to the original disposition of the room, the small niches of the wall have been brought back to light, and bronze and marble statuettes placed in them. On the wall, the small but grandiosely conceived *Madonna of the Caves* by Andrea Mantegna (fig. 44).

Room 18. « *Tribune* », built by Buontalenti (1585-89), and decorated with shells by Pocchetti. In the center, the famous *Medici Venus*, Roman copy of an original Hellenistic work of the end of the 4th century B.C., found in Hadrian's Villa in Rome. The other statues, also Roman copies of Greek exemplaries, represent: the *Knife Whetter*, the *Wrestlers*, and the *Dancing Faun*. In the niche of the Tribune is a cabinet of ebony with intarsiad Florentine mosaic. On the walls are splendid portraits of the Medici; among the most important, *Cosimo the Elder* by Pontormo (fig. 38); *Lorenzo the Magnificent*, by Vasari (fig. 39); *Lucrezia* (fig. 40) *and Bartolomeo Panciatichi*, by Bronzino, a refined portrait painter who also painted the portraits of *Cosimo I* and his wife *Eleanor of Toledo*, shown with her son *Giovanni*; by the same artist are the gracious children of Cosimo and Eleanor, don Garzia (fig. 41) and Isabella (fig. 42). Also of note in this room is the charming *Musical Angel* by Rosso Fiorentino.

Room 19. *Dedicated to Perugino and other artists of his group.* By Perugino we notice the two *Portraits of Vallombrosian Monks*, with warm chiaroscuro and intense spirituality; the famous *Young Man*, believed to be Alessandro Braccesi (fig. 43), and the large *Deposition*, with the vast Umbrian landscape that can be admired in the background. Observe the *Portrait of Evangelista Scappi* by Francesco Francia, pupil of Perugino; and by Lorenzo Costa, the *Portrait of Giovanni II Bentivoglio* and the small *St. Sebastian*. Here also can be seen two fragmentary paintings by Melozzo da Forlí showing the *Annunciation*, that was repainted on the back of *St. Benedict* and *St. John the Baptist*.

Room 20. *Dürer and the German painters.* Here are shown *Adam and Eve* by Lukas Cranach, influenced by Dürer. On the right, by Cranach, *Portrait of Martin Luther and his wife Catherine Bore* and the large *self-portrait*. On the following walls, portraits of *Luther*, of *Melantone*, and *Johann I* and *Friedrich II*, Electors of Saxony, also by Cranach, and the Portrait of *Ferdinand of Castille* by Hans Maler (16th century). By the great German painter and engraver Albrecht Dürer, who sojourned in Italy for a long time and felt the charm of the Venetians, we can admire a *Madonna and Child*, the *Portrait of his Father* (1490) and the celebrated *Adoration of the Magi* (1504 - fig. 45). Observe also the *St. Domenic* by the imaginative master and head of the Ferrarese school Cosmè Tura, and the 15th century copy of Dürer's *Adam and Eve,* conserved in the Prado of Madrid. On the wall, panels with *Stories of SS. Peter and Paul.* Also, a *landscape* by Hans Breughel, on the back of which is a *Calvary* taken from Dürer's engravings. On the ceiling, notice the Signoria, St. Maria Novella, and St. Croce Squares (St. Croce church without its actual façade).

Room 21. *Dedicated to Giovanni Bellini, to his pupil Giorgione and others of their school.* Here we can admire the famous *Allegory of Purgatory* (fig. 46) by Giovanni Bellini, inspired by a 13th century French poem, and a dramatic *Pietà* (datable circa 1490). Although in this work, color, the fundamental element of Bellini's painting, is absent, we can still observe the tonal sensitivity of his art, through the luminous and silvery rendering of the « grisaille ». Followed by the Apostles *St. Philip* and *St. James*, mature works of Dürer, who, after his contact with Bellini during his Venetian sojourn, developed his personality as a great artist. Cima da Conegliano, follower of Bellini, is present here with a *Madonna and Child*, with light and transparent colors. By Giorgione we admire the *Judgement of Solomon* and *Moses as a Child before the Pharoah*, extremely delicate works, rendered with an acute spirit of observation for the landscape (fig. 47). On the wall, tapestry of the *Deposition* executed by Nicholas Karcher (1594-1553), from a cartoon by Francesco Salviati. In the following room are other tapestries by the same authors, representing the *Ascension* and *Ecce Homo.* Observe on the wall above the tapestry, the war ruins around the Ponte Vecchio (1944), frescoed by the restorers after the liberation of the city.

Room 22. *Dedicated to the works of Flemish and German painters.* Together with the delicate works by the Flemish master Gerard

Fig. 45 - A. Dürer: Adoration of the Magi

Fig. 46 - Bellini: Allegory of Purgatory

David, are displayed paintings by the German artist Altdorfer, such as the *Departure* and the *Martyrdom of St. Florian*; followed by the portrait of *Sir Richard Southwell*, by Hans Holbein the Younger, painted during his sojourn in England. Also seen are other works by other Flemish and Dutch masters of the early 16th century.

Room 23. *Dedicated to Antonio Allegri called il Correggio*, an artist who unites echoes of Mantegna to a remarkable sensitivity of Leonardo's « sfumato » (shading). Among his works shown in this room we remember the famous *Virgin adoring the Child* (fig. 48). On the opposite wall, works by the Flemish painters Bernaert van Orley, Quentin Massys, and Joos van Cleve. On the successive walls, paintings by Leonardo's followers, among whom, Luini, Antonio Bazzi called il Sodoma, and an old copy of the *Madonna and Child*, from an original by Leonardo, conserved at the Louvre.

Room 24. Room of the Miniatures (generally closed). The room, delicately decorated in the 17th century, was destined to conserve jewels, that are now kept in the Pitti Palace. The room holds the valuable collection of miniatures on ivory and parchment by Italian and foreign artists. Notice the miniature of *Paolina Buonaparte*, Borghese Princess and Napoleon's sister, by the Swiss artist Counis, whose self-portrait is also shown.

Second Corridor, joining the two wings of the Uffizi. Observe the

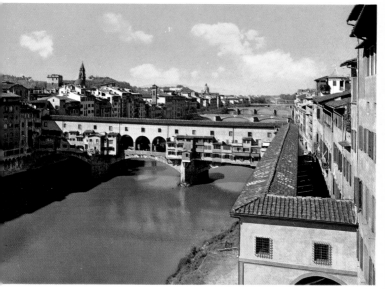

Fig. 47 - Giorgione: Moses as a Child
Fig. 48 - Correggio: Adoration of the Child
Fig. 49 - View of the Ponte Vecchio and the other bridges from the second
Corridor of the Uffizi Gallery

beautiful ceiling decorated in the 16th century. In the corridor are various classical sculptures, among which the *Boy taking a Thorn from his Foot*; a sarcophagus with a scene showing the *Fall of Phaeton*, Roman art of the II century; and the graceful *Girl Seated in the Act of Preparing to Dance*, Hellenistic copy (3rd century B.C.). From the central windows, a splendid view of Signoria Square, Palazzo Vecchio and the Duomo. From the lateral windows, view of the southern side of the city, with the hills of Bellosguardo, the bridges over the Arno (fig. 49), and the Vasarian corridor that, passing over the top of the Ponte Vecchio, reaches the Pitti Palace on the Boboli hillside to the left.

Third Corridor. Among the numerous classical statues and interesting Roman busts of the 3rd and 4th centuries, we notice at the beginning of the corridor, two statues representing *Mars Hanging*, Roman copies of original Greek works. On the walls, three series of tapestrires: first, of Florentine manufacture, from cartoons by Allori and Cigoli, showing *Scenes of the Passion of Christ*; the other two were made in Brussels and represent *Stories of Jacob* and *Battle scenes*. The beautiful ceiling, decorated with historical and mythological subjects by 17th century painters, was damaged during the last war like the other, and has been restored. After Room 25, the glass door opens on to the Vasarian Corridor (1564) that, after being damaged in 1944 and during the flood of 1966, has been largely restored. In the first section of this long corridor, a great part of the collection of self-portraits by Italian and foreign artists are displayed. To name a few are those of Titian, Andrea del Sarto, Vasari, Rubens, David, Ingres, Carot, Mancini, Canova etc. Raphael's self-portrait is shown in Room 25 together with his works.

Room 25. *Dedicated to Michelangelo, Raphael and their contemporaries.* From the works shown, we get a precise picture of the art of the two greatest masters of the Renaissance. Raphael Sanzio, who sums up in his style all the pictorial problems of his time, and introduces new solutions to painting, and Michelangelo Buonarrotti, who, with his only painting on wood, is the initiator of a « manner » that lasts for the entire century. On the wall, near the window, observe the *Portrait of Francesco Maria della Rovere*, young work by Raphael. On the next wall, *self-portrait* of the artist (fig. 50), and the *Madonna of the Goldfinch* with its beautiful Umbrian landscape from his Florentine period (c. 1507) (fig. 51). Dominating is the celebrated *Portrait of Pope Leo X* (1519 - fig. 52) seated between

Fig. 50 - Raffaello: Self-portrait
Fig. 51 - Raffaello: Madonna of the Goldfinch
Fig. 52 - Raffaello: Leo X among the Cardinals
Fig. 53 - Michelangelo: Holy Family

Cardinal Giulio (his cousin, later Pope Clement VII) on the left, and on the right, Luigi de' Rossi, secretary to both. Following is a *Portrait of Pope Julius II*, splendid old copy. On the next wall, between two works of Bronzino, we can admire the celebrated « tondo » containing Michelangelo's *Holy Family* (fig. 53) painted for the wedding of Agnolo Doni with Maddalena Strozzi (1504-1505). A rare and valuable painting in a spiral composition where, against a barely detectable landscape, the titanic artist placed powerful nude athletic figures, that preclude the frescoes of the Sistine Chapel. The sculptural group in the foreground renders the painting strongly dramatic. The beautiful frame with the Doni crests was executed by Domenico del Tasso following Michelangelo's design. Among the other works in the room is the famous *Visitation* by Albertinelli (1503 - fig. 54), perhaps painted in the period in which he was friend and collaborator of Fra' Bartolommeo. A large and solemn work, rendered with profound humanity, that influenced Raphael during his florentine sojourn. On the wall to the left of the door: *Joseph Presents his Father and Brothers to the Pharoah*, by Granacci; attributed to Raphael. Below, predella with the *Annunciation*, *Nativity* and *Presentation in the Temple* by Albertinelli.

Room 26. *Andrea d'Agnolo called Andrea del Sarto.* Among his works shown here is the well known *Madonna of the Harpies* (1517 - fig. 55), which gets its name from the small harpies that form the decoration of the pedestal on which the Madonna stands. A creation with soft chiaroscuro, and harmoniously composed figures. The room also contains works by Rosso Fiorentino and other mannerists, so called because they followed the « manner » of great artists, especially Michelangelo. Also shown are works by the Spanish artist Berruguete, who was in Italy to study the Florentine painters of the mannerist current. Temporarily, on easels, are displayed other works by Andrea del Sarto, belonging to altarpieces later dismantled.

Room 27. *Pontormo.* Jacopo Carrucci, born in Pontormo near Empoli (1494), a contemporary of Piero di Cosimo and Andrea del Sarto. He was influenced by Michelangelo and by Dürer's engravings, and became a mediate artist, creator of tormented and restless works, as shown here in his celebrated *Supper at Emmaus* (fig. 56). Among the other works in the room notice the predella with *Stories of St. Acacius*, by the Florentine Francesco Ubertini called il Bachiacca, genial designer of cartoons for tapestries; and the *Portrait of Pietro*

Fig. 54 - Albertinelli: Visitation

Fig. 55 - A. Del Sarto: Madonna of the Harpies

Fig. 56 - Pontormo: Supper at Emmaus

Carnesecchi by Puligo. The Sienese painter Beccafumi is duly represented with some of his works.

Room 28. *Dedicated to Titian*, the greatest Venetian artist of the 16th century, who brought the luminous tonality of Giovanni Bellini and Giorgione to the supreme height of color but was, at the same time, sensitive to Florentine and Roman expressions. Beginning from the right wall we have: *Portrait of Catherine Cornaro*, with the attributes of St. Catherine of Alexandria (old copy of a lost original). Following: *Flora*, live and passionate woman, rendered with intense color; *Venus of Urbino* (fig. 57), painted in 1538 for the Duke of Urbino, Ubaldo II della Rovere. This famous reclining Venus, with its vibrant color, is shown in a rich environment, made more realistic by the figures of the hand-maids looking for clothes. The light that penetrates from the window, limits the landscape and illuminates the room. Next, a *Knight of Malta*, at one time attributed to Giorgione, but now considered one of Titian's masterpieces, from the period when he was under the master's influence. By Palma il Vecchio, follower of Titian, we see the exuberant *Judith.* On the following walls: Portraits of *Francesco Maria della Rovere* and *Eleonora Gonzaga della Rovere*, Dukes of Urbino, by Titian. On the last wall the shapely *Venus and Cupid*, that Titian painted at the age of 73 years with the help of his pupils.

Room 29. *Parmigianino* (Francesco Mazzola da Parma 1503-1540). Refined painter of the Correggesque current who, aware of the Florentine and Roman styles, became the most original mannerist artist, as can be seen by his graceful *Madonna* called « *Of the Long Neck* » (fig. 58). The room also contains works by Dosso Dossi and Lucrezia Fontana from Bologna.

Room 30. *Dedicated to works of Niccolò dell'Abate and Battista Dossi*, together with other artists of his group, thus completing the panorama of Emilian painting.

Room 31. Contains a few works by Dossi and other Emilian and Venetian painters. From the window, a marvelous view of the Palazzo Vecchio, the Duomo and the nearby church of Orsanmichele on the left.

Room 32. *Sebastiano del Piombo and other Venetian artists.* On the central wall: the *Death of Adonis*, with a panorama of 16th century Venice in the background (fig. 59). Works of Sebastiano del Piombo, a Venetian of Giorgionesque formation, but active in Rome, who

Fig. 57 - Tiziano: Venus of Urbino

Fig. 58 - Parmigianino: Madonna of the Long Neck

Fig. 59 - Sebastiano del Piombo: Death of Adonis
Fig. 60 - Veronese: Holy Family with S. Barbara

75

Fig. 61 - Tintoretto: Leda and the Swan

was aware of the coloristic suggestions of Raphael and the plastic values of Michelangelo. On the next wall, *Sacred Conversation* by Lorenzo Lotto.

Room 33. Consists of a small corridor where we see a graceful antique Bacchus in the corner. Among the other works here are a *Self-portrait* by Antonio Moro (Flemish); *Christ bearing the Cross* by Morales (Spanish); and a *Portrait of Francis I King of France* by Clouet (French). Then, in the corridor itself, a *Medusa*, Flemish school of the 16th century, and small works by Florentine and Tuscan mannerists, among whom Ligozzi, Vasari, Allori, Zucchi and numerous other artists from this period. Finally, observe on the small back wall, the *Three Graces* by Poppi.

Room 34. *Paolo Veronese.* An artist expecially famous for the luminous and realistic rendering of the drapery. Among his works, the *Holy Family with St. Barbara* (fig. 60). The room contains three paintings by the great portrait painter G. Battista Moroni of Bergamo; *Portraits* by Campi of Cremona, the *Transfiguration* by Girolamo Savoldo of Brescia, and works of their period.

Fig. 62 - Rubens: Portrait of Isabella Brandt
Fig. 63 - Sustermans: Portrait of G. Galilei
Fig. 64 - Canaletto: View of Venice

Room 35. *Dedicated to Tintoretto* (Jacopo Robusti, 1519-94), Baroccio (Federico Fiori, 1528-1612) from Urbino, and Jacopo Bassano (c. 1515-92). With Tintoretto and Bassano, Venetian color arrives at true luministic painting as appears in *Leda and the Swan* (fig. 61) by Tintoretto. He is also great as a portrait painter, as is proven by the *Portrait of Jacopo Sansovino* shown here on the right. The formal elegance and the luminous research of Bassano are best realized in nocturnal and genre scenes, as shown in the *Roveto ardente* on the back wall. By Baroccio, artist of a complex formation, we can admire the grandiose *Madonna del Popolo.* The room also contains works by Leandro Bassano, lesser known follower of his father Jacopo, by the modest Domenico, son of the great Tintoretto, and by Palma the Younger, who continues Titian's heredity with that coloristic exuberance that identifies the early 17th century.

In the course of the reorganization works of the Gallery, the staircase of Buontalenti was opened, to which one accedes passing through a beautiful *Vestibule*, where are displayed a marble *wild-boar*, a bronze copy of which was made by Pietro Tacca for the fountain in the Straw Market, and the *Torso of a Satyr,* Greek art of the 2nd century A.D. Also shown are elegant Medicean tapestries. The narrow staircase leads to the Loggia of the Uffizi, therefore it is used as an exit.

Room 41. *Dedicated to Rubens* (1577-1640). Heroic and passionate personality, formed in Rome and Venice, he reaches the height of expression on his return to Antwerp (1608). We can admire his large canvases of *Henry IV at the Battle of Ivry, Triumphant Entry of Henry IV into Paris,* and the small *Portrait of his wife Isabella Brandt* (fig. 62), a work of pleasant and poetic intimacy. Of Rubens' school notice the *Portrait of Galileo Galilei* (fig. 63), by Sustermans, Flemish painter active at the Medici court; *Portrait of Giovanni di Montfort,* by Van Dyck, and, by the Genoese Gaulli called il Baciccio, the *Portrait of Cardinal Leopold de' Medici.*

Room 42. *Room of Niobe* (temporary arrangement). This room was made by Grand Duke Pietro Leopold of Lorraine, who commissioned the architect Gasparre M. Paoletti to build it (1777-80) to hold the group of *Niobe and her Children,* Roman copy of an original Hellenistic work of the III-II cent. B.C. The style of the architecture is neo-classic. The group of statues was found in Rome in 1583. The room temporarily holds works that were in rooms 36-40, such as the *Views of Venice* (fig. 64) by Canaletto, and those more pictoresque

Fig. 65 - Guardi: View of Venice
Fig. 66 - Caravaggio: Medusa
Fig. 67 - Caravaggio: Young Baccus

Fig. 68 - Rembrandt: Portrait of an Old Man

by Guardi (fig. 65). The room also contains works by Magnasco, Rosalba Carriera and other artists of that period. Also shown here 18th century French works including the *Daughters of Louis XV* by Nattier; graceful works by Watteau, Chardin and others. In the center of the room is a *marble vase* of the 3rd century belonging to the Medici collection. The walls of this splendid room are enriched by Medicean tapestries representing *episodes from the Lives of the Medici Grand Dukes*, and, on the opposite wall, *Stories of Moses*.

Room 43. Dedicated to the famous *landscapes* by Ruysdael and to the works of Van Mieris, Jan Steen, Cornel Palemberg and other Dutch masters, who show a minute and analytical attention in representing the vast and melancholic landscape characteristic of their country (fig. 57).

Room 44. *With works by Annibale Carracci, Crespi, Guido Reni and others.* Here we can admire the *Medusa* (fig. 66) by Caravaggio (Michelangelo Merisi from Caravaggio near Bergamo, 1573-1610), great innovator of Italian painting who also exercised an enormous influence on European painting of the 17th century, and even left traces of influence on the art of the great Dutchman Rembrandt, present here with his celebrated *Portrait of an Old Man* (fig. 68), and two *selfportraits*, one juvenile and one at a mature age. By Caravaggio we also have the famous *Young Bacchus* (fig. 67). Observe then the works of Aannibale Carracci, of whom are shown the *Portrait of a Monk*, a *Man with a Monkey*, and a *Baccante*. By Giuseppe M. Crespi we have graceful scenes of the *Painter's Family, The Flea* and a *Pastoral scene*. By Francesco Albani: *Dance of the Putti, Summer Sports*. By Guidi Reni, *Portrait of a Dominican Friar.*

CHURCH OF ORSANMICHELE (fig. 69)
(On Via Calzaiuoli, near Signoria Square; map of monuments n. 9)

It was the former oratory of San Michele in Orto. In 1290 Arnolfo di Cambio built the "Loggia del Grano" (Grain Market), destroyed by a fire (1304). The cube shaped church, typical example of Florentine Gothic, was built by Francesco Talenti and Neri di Fioravanti (1337-1404), who built the grain lodge in the upper floors, in case of famine or seige of the city, now a hall used for periodic expositions by the Superintendant of Arts. In 1387 Simone Talenti closed the arches on the ground floor of the church in order to make the famous niches containing the statues of the patron saints of the Florentine guilds.

Fig. 69 - Church of Orsanmichele - Lower floors

The main entrance is from Via dell'Arte della Lana, but one can enter from the small door facing Via Calzaiuoli, from where, beginning from left to right, we can admire: 1) Tabernacle of the Mercanti di Calimala (Guild of Foreign Wool Merchants) – *St. John the Baptist* by Ghiberti (1414-1416), with harmonious late-Gothic rythym; 2) Tabernacle of the Tribunal of the Merchants, by Donatello and Michelozzo: famous bronze group of the *Incredulity of St. Thomas* by Andrea del Verrocchio (1464-1483); above, medallion by Luca della Robbia. 3) Tabernacle of the Judges and Notaries: *St. Luke*, by Giambologna (1601). North side, Via Orsanmichele, 1) Tabernacle of the Butchers: *St. Peter*, young work by Donatello (1408-1413). 2) Tabernacle of the Tanners Guild: *St. Philip*, by Nanni di Banco (1409-1411). 3) Tabernacle of the Carpenters and Masons: *Four crowned Saints* and relief representing architects and

Figg. 70-71 - Orcagna: Tabernacle, Death and Assumption of the Virgin

sculptors, work of Nanni di Banco (1408); above medallion by Luca della Robbia. 4) Tabernacle of the Armourers and Sword makers, statue in bronze of *St. George*, copy of the original in marble by Donatello, conserved in the National Museum. Observe on the base, *St. George who frees the Princess* by Donatello, highly pictorial bas-relief. On the right, *Palace of the Arte della Lana* (Guild of the Wool Workers), restored in 1905 for the Dante Society, and joined to the upper floors of the church by means of the corridor. This tower house was the seat of the powerful Wool Guild, that employed about 30,000 workers and had 200 shop. The tabernacle on the corner ith the *Incoronation of the Virgin,* XIV cent. work by Jacopo del Casentino, was transferred here in 1895, following the demolition of the old center. Following on the west side, facing Via Arte della Lana: 1) Tabernacle of the Moneychangers: *St. Matthew*, bronze by Ghiberti (1420). Over the main door of the church, sculpture by Nicolò Lamberti. 2) Tabernacle of the Wool Workers: *St. Stephen*, bronze by Ghiberti (1426). 3) Tabernacle of the Blacksmiths: *St. Eligius*, by Nanni di Banco (1415); on the base an episode in the life of the Saint is represented.

South side facing Via de' Lamberti: 1) Tabernacle of the Linen Workers: *St. Mark*, powerful work of Donatello (1408-1413). 2) Tabernacle of the Furriers; statue of *St. James*, perhaps work of

Figs. 72-73 - Daddi: Madonna - Sangallo: St. Ann, Madonna and Child

Nicolò di Pietro Lamberti, in the bas-relief, *Beheading of the Saint*, attributed to Ciuffagni. 3) Tabernacle of the Doctors and Apothecaries, by Simone Talenti; *Madonna of the Roses* perhaps by Simone Ferrucci. 4) Tabernacle of the Silk-workers and Goldsmiths: *St. John the Evangelist*, bronze by Baccio da Montelupo (1515). Above, in the *Medallion*, putto and crest of this guild, by Andrea della Robbia, beloved nephew and faithful pupil of Luca, father of Giovanni.

Interior of the Church (fig. 70), rectangular shaped, conserved in its original structure, illuminated by XV cent. stained glass windows. Solid pilasters, with frescoed heads, support the harmonious vaults and separate the lateral naves. In the right nave is the famous *Tabernacle* by Andrea di Cione called Orcagna (1349-59) (for illumination ask the custodian). This admirable Gothic work terminates on high with the little cupola with the relief of the Savior. The altar, with small twisted columns is adorned with panels on the bottom, and enriched with polychrome mosaic scenes from the *Life of the Virgin*.

On the back of the altar is a large scene of the *Death and Ascension of the Virgin* (fig. 71) by Orcagna, of obvious Sienese inspiration. The small spiraled columns and the *Angels carrying candelabras* of the parapet are by Pietro del Migliore (1366). The altar-piece with the famous *Madonna and Child* (fig. 72) is by Bernardo Daddi (1366).

Fig. 74 - Piazza del Duomo with the Baptistry, Giotto's Bell-Tower, the Cathedral (St. Mary of the Flower). In the background the Dome designed by Brunelleschi.

On the altar, to the left, *St. Ann with the Virgin and Child* (fig. 73), marble group by Francesco da Sangallo (1526).
Going out on to Via Calzaiuoli, on the opposite side of the street

is the CHURCH OF S. CARLO DEI LOMBARDI, attributed to Neri di Fioravante and Benci di Cione.

Inside, on the high altar is a *Deposition* by Nicolò di Pietro Gerini (end of XIV cent.). Continuing on the left of Via Calzaiuoli (widened in 1842) we reach the nearby Piazza del Duomo where, on the corner, is the beautiful LOGGIA DEL BIGALLO, jewel of Florentine architecture, attributed to Arnoldi (1352). The wrought-iron gate is by the Sienese Petrucci (1358). Inside the Loggia is a tabernacle with the *Madonna, Child and Angels* by Noferi (1515). In the lunette (on the Baptistry side) *Madonna and Child* by Alberto Arnoldi (1361).

PIAZZA DUOMO (Cathedral Square)

In this vast square, also incorporating S. Giovanni Square, which is the ideal religious center of the city, are located the Baptistry, the Cathedral and the beautiful Bell Tower (fig. 75). We point out that, for the civic numeration, the side of the Baptistry and the Archiepiscopal Palace is S. Giovanni Square, while the side of the Cathedral, Bell Tower and Misericordia is Piazza Duomo.

THE BAPTISTRY

Dedicated to St. John the Baptist, patron of the city. This splendid Romanesque building of the XI cent. that Dante called "the beautiful St. John", covered with white and green marble, is enriched by three magnificent bronze doors. The usual entrance is on the South side. In order to follow the stylistic evolution of the sculpture of the three doors, we suggest they be visited in the order shown ahead.

Interior. It is octagonal shaped, harmonious and solemn, covered, as on the exterior, with green and white marble (fig. 75). The cupola is enriched with *mosaics* that are also used in the vault of the apse, added in the XII cent. Solid and old columns, some of porphyry, support the trabeated architecture. Above is the gallery with exquisite mullioned windows that, with the lantern, illuminate the interior. In the cupola let us admire the famous mosaics, begun by Jacopo Francescano (1225) and continued by Venetian and Florentine artists, among whom is believed to be the young Cimabue who, beginning with the cartoons for these mosaics, laid the basis of Florentine painting.

Particularly interesting is the large and majestic figure of the *Savior in the Final Judgement*. Represented in the other areas are *celestial Hierarchies*; episodes of the Bible among which the *Creation of Adam and Eve, Stories of Joseph* and of *St. John the Baptist*, patron of Florence.

The large baptismal font that was in the center and where Dante was baptized, was dismantled in 1577. The fragments are conserved in the Museo del Duomo. Now baptism is performed at the small font against the wall, of the Pisan school (1371), surmounted by the *Baptism of Christ* by Allori (1590). Observe the area of the floor intarsied with motives of the Zodiac and oriental designs. On the opposite wall: *Tomb of the Antipope John XXIII* (Baldassare Cossa) deposed by the Council of Constance which recognized the sovereignty of Pope Martin V, who subsequently named him Cardinal of Florence, where he died in 1419. Cosimo the Elder, his great patron, commissioned Donatello to do this masterpiece which he executed with the help of other artists, among whom was Michelozzo, author of the exquisite figures of *Faith, Hope* and *Charity* in the lower niches.

Fig. 75 - Baptistry - Interior
Fig. 76 - South Door - Andrea Pisano: Hope
Fig. 76 bis - North Door - Lorenzo Ghiberti: Annunciation

To the left, monumental slab of Bishop Ranieri (XII cent.). The altar of the tribune was reconstructed in the XII cent. The *angel candelabra* is by Agostino di Jacopo (1320). At the back of the apse, *Statue of the Baptist* by Piamontini (1688). To the left of the tribune, between two sarcofagi, was the famous *penitant Mary Magdalen* in polychromal wood by Donatello (1460) restored from the damage received during the flood of 1966.

Fig. 77 - Lorenzo Ghiberti: Second door of the Baptistry called "Gates of Paradise". Gilded bronze panel showing episodes from the Old Testament.

South Door. By Andrea Pisano (da Pontedera) (1330-1336) who executed them following suggestions (it is believed) of Giotto, his teacher. The door has 20 panels with *Scenes from the Life of St. John the Baptist* and the *Cardinal Virtues*. They are of gothic rhythm as can be seen in the plastic and harmonious scenes of *Herod's Banquet* and the *Deposition of the Baptist in the Tomb* which, together with the panel representing *Hope* (fig. 76), announce the style of the first doors of Ghiberti, on the opposite side. The frames of the portal were later enriched with *leaves* and *graceful Angel's heads* by Vittorio Ghi-

1) Creation of Adam and Eve, Original Sin, Expulsion of Adam and Eve from the Garden of Eden; 2) Stories of Noah; 3) Stories of Jacob and Esau; 4) Moses receives the tables of the Law on Mt. Sinai; 5) Battle against the Philistines, David defeats Goliath; 6) Cain and Abel working the fields, Slaying of Abel; 7) The Apparition of the Angels to Abraham, Sacrifice of Isaac; 8) Joseph is sold to the Merchants, the gold cup is discovered in Benjamin's sack, Joseph makes himself known to his brothers; 9) The people of Israel cross the Jordan, the Battle of Jerico; 10) Solomon receives the Queen of Sheba at the Temple.

berti, son and pupil of Lorenzo (1452-1462). Above the architrave, the *Beheading of St. John the Baptist* is by Vincenzo Danti (1572). Continuing to the left of the Baptistry, observe at the end of the Square, the Archiepiscopal Palace, built by Dosio (1572), rebuilt farther back in 1895 to enlarge the square.

From this side we can see the apse of the Baptistry, added in the XII cent. Farther ahead in the square, the *Column of St. Zenobius*, erected to commemorate the miracle of the Saint that, according to tradition, made a dead tree burst into flower when his remains passed by as they were being transfered from S. Lorenzo to the Duomo on January 23, 429.

North Door of the Baptistry. By Lorenzo Ghiberti (winner of the celebrated contest of 1402 in which great artists such as Jacopo della Quercia and Brunelleschi participated). Ghiberti, with the help of numerous collaborators, among whom Paolo Uccello and Donatello, began this first door in 1403, finishing them in 1424. The twenty upper panels narrate *Stories of the New Testament* while the lower eight represent *Evangelists and Doctors of the Church.* The most recent anti-traditional critics find in this door (ignored by many), more personal characteristics than in the second door, where the artist introduces the bas-relief inspired by Donatello. Here the scenes of rhythmic Gothic modulation, are rendered with more profound poetry os shown in the panels of the *Temptantion and the Annunciation* (fig. 76 bis). Observe, in the frame work and in the bands around the panels, the graceful heads of youths and adults. In the middle band on the left, the fifth head down from the top, with the turban, is a self portrait of Ghiberti. On the architrave, the bronze group of *John the Baptist preaching to a Pharisee and a Levite*, work of Gian Francesco Rustici (1506-1511), who shows the influence of Leonardo.

Second Door. Opposite to the Cathedral, called "Gate of Paradise" (fig. 77), was also done by Ghiberti (1425-1452) who completed it after 27 years of work, with the help of his son Vittorio, Bernardo Cennini, Michelozzo and other artists, including Benozzo Gozzoli. It is the door that Michelangelo judged worthy to be the Gate of Paradise. After the last war it was cleaned and brought back to its original gilded aspect.

In the panels of this famous work we can admire ample compositions rich with figures, architecture and landscapes, done in bold, medium and bas-reliefs, typical of the great Renaissance era. The subjects of the ten panels, suggested by the humanist Leonardo Bruni, and taken from the *Old Testament* represent, beginning with the top left panel and reading from left to right:

1) Creation of Adam and Eve, Original Sin, Expulsion of Adam and Eve from the Garden of Eden; 2) Cain and Abel working the fields, Slaying of Abel; 3) Stories of Noah, rendered with richness of details; 4) The Apparition of the Angels to Abraham, Sacrifice of Isaac; 5) Stories of Jacob and Esau particularly interesting for its architectural, plastic and Renaissance values; 6) Joseph is sold to the Merchants, the gold cup is discovered in Benjamin's sack, Joseph makes himself known to his brothers; 7) Moses receives the tables of the Law on Mt. Sinai; 8) The people of Israel cross the Jordan, the Battle of Jericho; 9) Battle against the Philistines, David defeats Goliath; 10) Solomon receives the Queen of Sheba at the Temple.

In the framework of the door are graceful figures of Sybils alternated with small heads portraying Florentine figures of the era. In the central vertical band, in the lower half, the small bald head is the selfportrait of a mature Ghiberti. On the architrave, the *Baptism of Christ* is by Andrea Sansovino 1502; the *Angel* is by Spinazzi (XVII cent.). At the sides of door are two old porphyre columns, donated to the Florentines by the Pisans (1117) for having faithfully defended their city while Pisa was at war in the Balearic Isles.

THE CATHEDRAL - SANTA MARIA DEL FIORE
(Saint Mary of the Flower)

Arnolfo di Cambio began the construction (1296) to replace the old
church of St. Reparata. After Arnolfo's death (1302), the work was
continued by Giotto who died in 1337. Later (1357) Francesco
Talenti and Giovanni di Lapo Ghini continued its construction, en-
larging the original plan. In 1412 the name Santa Reparata was
changed to S. Maria del Fiore (St. Mary of the Flower), alluding
to the Florentine fleur-de-lys. In 1436, when Brunelleschi completed
the cupola, the Church was consecrated by Pope Eugenius IV.

Façade by Emilio de Fabris (1881-88) is a cold XIX cent. imitation
of Glorentine Gothic, inspired by the decoration of sides of the
Cathedral. The bronze doors with *Stories of the Virgin* are by; Pas-
aglia (1897-1903), that on the left and the one in the center; and
by Cassioli (1899), the door on the right.

Interior (fig. 78). The church is in the form of a Latin cross and

PLAN OF THE CATHEDRAL
(St. Mary of the Flower)

1. Bust of Brunelleschi
2. Statue of Isaiah, by Nanni di Banco (1408)
3. Bust of Giotto
4. Holy water basin (1380). The Angel and the basin are copies of the original in the Duomo Museum
5. Bust of Marsilio Ficino
6. Choir
7. Terracotta by Luca della Robbia
8. Old Sacristy
9. Reliquary of St. Zenobius (Lorenzo Ghiberti)
10. Bronze door and terracotta by Luca della Robbia
11. New Sacristy
12. Pietà by Michelangelo
13. Entrance to the dome
14. Domenico Michelino: Dante shedding light of Florence with his Divine Comedy (plate 34)

Fig. 78 - The Cathedral: Interior

has three naves (length 153 meters, width 38 meters, width of the transept 90 meters). It is the third longest church in the world after St. Peter's in Rome and St. Paul's in London. The first impression of nude semplicity devoid of any decoration gives way to admiration, for the controlled and measured proportions, which differs from the other nordic cathedrals. The vertical surge of the vaults is broken by the gallery, that runs above the arches continuing under the cupola and measured proportions, which differs from the other nordic cathedrals. The vertical surge of the vaults is broken by the gallery, that runs above the arches continuing under the cupola and along the transept. The space in the arms of the transept is enriched by lateral domed chapels.

The very ample and architecturally weel defined space, is sustained by simple and solid pilasters, typical example of Italianized Gothic. The light penetrates from the large rose window of the central nave and through the tall slim windows of the lateral naves.

Limiting ourselves to the most important works, we point out, on the internal façade: Stained glass window, following a design by Ghiberti. Around the clock are heads of Prophets by Paolo Uccello. In the right nave, *bust of Brunelleschi*, work of Bugggiano his student and heir. *Wooden tabernacle with Statue of Prophet* by Nanni di Banco (1408). *Bust of Giotto*, by Benedetto da Maiano. Recently,

Fig. 79 - **Michelangelo: Pietà** At present in the Museum of the Cathedral Institution

remains of the pre-existent church of Santa Reparata were brought
to light. Found were the walls, some frescoes, pieces of a wall decoration in brick and little columns, monumental slabs of the early

XIV. cent. as well as the Tomb of Filippo Brunelleschi. Moving far ther ahead in the right nave, in the niche near the side door is the *Bust of the Philosopher Marsilio Ficino* (d. 1499) by Andrea Ferrucci The *octagonal marble Choir*, with bas-reliefs of *Apostles* and *Prophet* is a masterpiece by Bandinelli and helpers (1555). On high, th *Wooden Crucifix* is by Benedetto da Maiano. On the solid wings o the transept with its massive pillars, Brunelleschi's cupola rises ele gantly and majestically (height 114 meters), inspiring that of Rom and of St. Paul's in London. The ingenious artists, after studying th monuments of ancient Rome, including the Pantheon, realized thi splendid cupola with a new spirit, however conserving the Gothi idea that Arnolfo certainly had in mind when he projected the XII century construction.

With machines of his own invention, Brunelleschi hauled the material on high and built the octagonal cupola, two vaults separated by an air-space (as shown in the diagram-design A) that, solidly sustained by the play of weight and counter-weight, rises ever higher "between the sky and the earth". The decoration of the interior was supposed to be mosaic but was unfortunately altered by Vasari and Zuccari who frescoed the pompous and manneristic *Final Judgement* (1572- 79). The magnificent *stained glass windows* around the base of the dome were made from cartoons by Donatello, Paolo Uccello, Ghi- berti and Andrea del Castagno. In the niches of the wings around the choir are figures of *Apostles* by XV cent. sculptors; among the most notable, *St. James* by Jacopo Sansovino. On the right of the choir is the *door to the old Sacristy*. In the lunette, the *Ascension* in glazed terracotta, by Luca della Robbia c. 1450).

At the back of the apse (n. 9 on the plan), under the altar (often covered), is the famous bronze reliquary by Ghiberti (1442), with the *Miracle of St. Zenobius who Resuscitates a Child in the Presence of his Mother and Onlookers*. Above the altar, a mediocre *Last Supper* by Balducci (XVI cent.). Returning toward the transept one can admire the architectural complex of the church. On the right, the bronze door of the new Sacristy, by Luca della Robbia, with panels representing: *the Madonna and Child with Evangelists and Doctors of the Church*. Observe the self-portrait of the artist in the small bald head below. The splendid *Resurrection* in the lunette, of glazed terracotta, is also a masterpiece by Luca della Robbia.

Interior of the Sacristy. Contains cabinets with intarsia decoration enriched with festoons, due in great part to the brothers da Maiano. There are two marble lavaboes by Buggiano (1440): the delicate *angel's head* on the right one is attributed to Mino da Fiesole. Lo- renzo the Magnificent found cover in this Sacristy while his brother Giuliano fell under the assassin's knife, in the Pazzi Conspiracy

g. 80 - Domenico Michelino: Dante illuminating the City with his Divine
omedy - Cathedral

95

(Easter 1478). Leaving here, to the right is Michelangelo's *Piet* (1550 - fig. 79) that was intended for his own tomb. It is an in complete work of intense drama. In the face of *Joseph of Arimathea* who supports the body of Christ, is Michelangelo's self portrait. Th artist, perhaps in a moment of discouragement, damaged the group that was later recomposed by his pupil Calcagni, who finished th figure of Mary Magdalen.

On the floor in the center of the transept, observe the *Gnomo.* represented by the metal disc that was placed here in 1450 b Toscanelli for the purpose of controlling the center of gravity of th cupola on the day if the summer solstice. Continuing along the righ nave, before the lateral door, is a small door of the entrance to th Cupola. For aesthetic reasons it is not consented to install an elevato for a comfortable ascent to the cupola but, to those that are able, w do suggest climbing the interesting spiral stair-case to admire, fron above, the beautiful geometric polychromed marble floor of th church, by Baccio d'Agnolo (1526), the ingenious internal construc tion of the cupola, and the vast panorama of the city and its surround ing hills. Continuing our walk in the church, on the wall, *Dant shedding light on Florence with his Divine Comedy*, painting b Domenico Michelino (fig. 80), pupil of Fra' Angelico (plate XL) Farther ahead are two admirable *equestrian portraits* of the Floren tine Republic's most faithful generals; *John Hawkwood*, by Paol

Brunelleschi, friend the astronomer Tosca nelli, after his profoun mathematical studies an attentive observations c ancient buildings, esp cially the Pantheon i Rome, built the first cu pola without use of th customary scaffolding. A shown in the sketch, hi creation is a doubl dome, the outer one hav ing enormous ribs. Belo big robust pilaster around the tribune pr pare the remarkabl thrust of the cupol that rises elegantly an majestically on high.

ccello (1436) who inspired Andrea del Castagno (1456), author of
e other General, *Nicolò da Tolentino*. The two frescoes at one
me were on the internal façade, but then were restored, transferred
to canvas, and displayed here in the better light.

the last bay is a *bust* of Arnolfo di Cambio (1843); in the wooden
bernacle, statue of a prophet, portrait of the humanist Poggio Brac-
olini (school of Donatello). Finally, *a bust of Emilio de Fabris*,
e architect of the façade, by Consani (1887).

mong the events that took place in this Cathedral we remember:
e Council of Florence, that reconciled the Greek and Latin
urches under the patronage of Cosimo the Elder (1429). During
e Lenten season of 1497, Savonarola gave his memorable sermons,
hich influenced the course of Florentine history and the artists of
e time.

IOTTO'S BELL-TOWER

was erected on line with the façade of the Cathedral and enriched
ith white, pink and green marble. It is 84,75 meters in height and
is a staircase with 416 steps. It is a splendid example of Floren-
ne Gothic architecture, square formed and placed on solid lateral
lasters. It was begun by Giotto in 1334, who completed the first
ne. After his death (1337) it was continued by his pupil Andrea
isano who worked on the two upper stories with the beautiful
ullioned windows. In 1348 he was succeded by Talenti who finish-
i it in 1359. There is still discussion about Giotto's original project
rminating with cusps that Talenti changed by ending with a pano-
mic terrace that has an open-work parapet and a jutting cornice
sting on corbelling and trilobated arches. In order to have a better
ok at the bell-tower we suggest you stand at a distance from where
u can see the highest mullioned window, placed in the arch of the
sp, that harmonizes with the small door on the bottom. The statues
f Saints and Prophets, including Donatello's *Abacus*, that there once
the niches, are now conserved in the Cathedral Museum, together
ith the panels of the base representing *Scenes from Genesis* and the
ctivities of *Man*, by Andrea Pisano following designs by Giotto,
hich have been substituted with plaster models.

o the right of the Bell-tower across the street:

:AT AND ORATORY OF THE MISERICORDIA

mong the oldest congregations in Italy, it was founded by a simple porter
r the purpose of transporting the sick to hospitals. The "brothers", that belong
all circles, take turns, without compensation, in offering this service and other
orks of charity.

Exterior of the Cathedral. Moving along on this side of the street, we can bett admire the "beautiful" Bell-tower and the majestic architectural complex of tl Cathedral, enlarged in the course of the centuries, as shown by the splend mullioned windows, of which the smaller and lower ones on the left obvious belong to the original plan. Among the most beautiful **portals** on this side, v point out the one on the right near the cupola called of the "Canonici", by L renzo di Giovanni d'Ambrogio and Piero di Giovanni Tedesco. In the lunet the *Madonna and Child* is by Lorenzo di Giovanni d'Ambrogio who, wit Nicolò Lamberti, also sculpted the two *Angels*. We suggest you proceed towai Via del Proconsolo and Via dell'Orivolo, in order to better admire the Bel tower, the solid base of the Cupola, and the gallery that runs along only oi section of it, by Baccio d'Agnolo, left incomplete because it was criticized t Michelangelo, who defined it a "cricket cage". On the corner of Via Orivolo the beautiful *Strozzi of Mantova Palace* (XVI cent.) with its rusticated stom beautiful windows and splendid portals.

Continuing around the square we see the entrance to the Cathedral Museum th we describe ahead. Also observe the portals of the "workshops" that numbere many in this square. Among these is that of Donatello indicated by the modei bust in the niche. After Via dei Servi, observe, on the side of the Cathedral, tl famous door called of the "mandorla" (almond) because of the shape of tl niche containing the beautiful sculpture of the "*Assumption*", by Nanni Banco. The small figures of *Prophets* on the long pilasters are believed to be t the young Donatello. The mosaic representing the "Annunciation" is by Dom nico Ghirlandaio with the help of his brother David. Retracing our steps to n. of the Piazza Duomo, is the entrance to the

Fig. 81 - Museum of the Opera del Duomo - Donatello: Choir - loft (detail)

USEO DELL'OPERA DEL DUOMO (Cathedral Museum)
aint Mary of the Flower)

1 the niche above the entrance is a *bust of Cosimo I*, work of Ban-
ini (1572). Access to the Museum is through the atrium. On the left,
e three small rooms are dedicated to the models of the cupola
id the façade of the Cathedral by various artists and also contains
runelleschi's death-mask.

1 the large rectangular room are works by Arnolfo di Cambio
. 1302), architect and sculptor, including, on the left, the statue of
ope Boniface VIII with his arm raised in blessing, and on the op-
osite wall, statues that were on the old façade of the Cathedral.
gainst the right wall, among other statues is Donatello's *St. John
e Evangelist*, that was supposed to have inspired Michelangelo
ith his Moses. On the wall, observe the design for the old façade
the Cathedral, dismantled in the XVI cent. The room farther
ead is dedicated to *valuable missals* and *sacred vestments* that,
ith the rare reliquaries of the little chapel to the left, were badly
imaged during the flood of 1966. On the right of the room, in the
nall corridor, are fragments of the antique *baptismal font* where
ante was baptized and that was in the Baptistry. The brief stair-
se leads to the

irst Floor, dedicated to the famous choir lofts by Luca della Robbia
428-31) and Donatello (1433-39) (fig. 81). On the left, above, is
e plaster reconstruction of Luca's cantoria with *figures of children*

Figs. 84-85 - Museum of the Opera del Duomo - Luca della Robbia: Choi - loft (detail)

singing psalm 31 of David. Below are the dismantled original panel (figs. 84-85). On the right wall is *Donatello's choir loft* with dancing putti, rendered impetuous and spontaneous, in their natural and naïve mannerisms. On the walls are *Florentine tapestries* with Stories c *St. John the Baptist*, from cartoons by Alessandro Allori (XVI cent.)

Among the statues originally in the nichehs of the Bell-tower notice against the end wall, the famous Abakuk (fig. 82) by Donatello rendered with bitter realism. On the right we enter the room with the famous silver altar, once in the Baptistry, a masterpiece by XV cent. Florentine artists. In the center of the altar are *episodes o the life of the Baptist* by Cennini and the figure of *St. John* by Michelozzo. On the left side, the *Birth of St. John* by Antonio Pollaiuolo and the *Visitation* by Bernardo Cennini. On the right side *Herod's Banquet* by Antonio Salvi and *Beheading of the Saint* by Verrocchio. In this room also are precious embroideries with 27 little scenes of the *Life of Christ* and, in the showcase against the entrance wall is a rare Byzantine mosaic with scenes of *Christ's Life* (XIII cent.).

Returning to the room with the Choir-lofts, we pass into the small room dedicated to the famous panels, originally on the Bell-tower by Andrea Pisano. It is believed that some of the preparatori design for these panels were furnished by Giotto. Notice the ones of *"Agri culture"* and *"the Drunkenness of Noah"* (fig. 83) that reval th superior personality of Giotto as a sculptor.

SECOND ITINERARY

Church of San Lorenzo, Laurentian Library, Medici Chapels - Medici-Riccardi Palace - Church of St. Mark, Museum of St. Mark, of Angelico - Accademy Gallery, Tribune of David - Conservatory of Music "Cherubini" - Museo delle Pietre Dure (Manufactory of Mosaics).
This itinerary is indicated on the monumental map by the numbers 4, 5, 7, and 8).

CHURCH OF SAN LORENZO

In the square (fig. 86, city plan 4), on a beautiful base, is the *monument* to Giovanni father of Cosimo I, by Bandinelli (1540), with the unusual figure of a seated general. This monument tauched the wittiness of the Florentines, who joined the famous epigram: Messer Giovanni delle Bande Nere, "annoyed and tired from his long journey, dismounted from his horse and took a seat". Notice the base, more interesting than the statue, adorned with Medicean heraldic motives. The Church was built on commission of Cosimo the Elder (in the place of a preexisting church believed to have been founded by St. Ambrose) near his Palace, as a parish church and Medicean cemetery. It is the first Renaissance church, begun by Brunelleschi in 1419 (upon return from his studies of Roman basilicas) and finished by his pupil Manetti. Later Michelangelo made a project for the façade but it was never carried out.

By Michelangelo is the internal façade of the church and the famous Laurentian Library in the cloister. The bell-tower is by Ruggeri (1746).

Fig. 86 - Church of San Lorenzo and the Medici Chapels

101

Interior. It is in the form of a Latin cross with three naves and a wide transept with chapels along the walls. The wide central nave with the panelled cailing and the geometrically patterned floor, is illuminated by large rectangular windows. In the lateral naves with the cross vaulted ceiling, the light enters through small round windows.

This harmonious basilica is a triumph of Brunelleschi's perpective vision. The grey stone ribs and columns, with their capitals topped by elegant abacuses that support the round arches, perfectly harmonize with the white plaster walls. At the end of the central nave as seen on the plan marked nos. 2-3, are the famous *pulpits* bu Donatello, made in collaboration with his helpers Bertoldo and Bellano with panels representing the Passion of Christ. Particularly interesting is the *Deposition* in the left pulpit, the last work of the artist rendered with profound humanity. At the head of the right transep (behind the pulpit no. 4 on the plan), is an exquisite *tabernacle* with graceful "putti" by Desiderio da Settignano, which was the inspiration for many other famous Florentine tabernacles.

In the chapel of the right transept is the tomb of the Naturalis Stenson. (We point out that the Main Chapel was shortened when the Chapel of the Princes was built, attaching it to the church, as described ahead [see plan]).

Main Altar, enclosed by a balustrade. The altar is decorated with semi-precious stones. The marble *Crucifix* is by Baccio da Montelupo pupil of Michelangelo. In front of the balustrade observe the metal gratings marking the place under which Cosimo the Elder (d. 1464) is buried. Next to him is buried Donatello, for whom Cosimo was a great patron and admirer.

At the head of the left transept a large but overpowering fresco of the Martyrdom of St. Lawrence by Bronzino, who, having returned from Rome, wanted to emulate Michelangelo's art in the Vatican. The bautiful *Choir-loft* inlaid with quartz and polychrome marble i attributed to Donatello. In the chapel to the left, *St. Joseph in his workshop with the Child Jesus*, work of intense humanity by Annigoni, the famous portrait painter of Popes and Sovereigns. In the last chapel of this left transept is the *Monument to the Countess Moltk Ferrari Corbelli* by Duprè (1864). On the left we enter the

Old Sacristy, by Brunelleschi (1420-29). It is square formed and the light penetrates from the lantern of the little cupola and from the large lateral lunettes. The apse, with its fine marble balustrade has an altar made by Donatello's pupils, following the master's design.

On High, the cupola is enriched by frescoed *Signs of the Zodiac*

On two sides of the apse are: two *Doors* with small ionic columns and a triangular tympanum by Donatello into which the artist inserted his valuable bronze doors with panels representing *the Apostles and Doctors of the church* rendered intensely dramatic. By this great sculptor, who was also a friend and collaborator of Brunelleschi, we can admire: the *Stories of St. John the Evangelist*, in the pendentives; *the Four Evangelists,* in terracotta in the lunettes; and the lively *Cherubs* around the trabeation.

Donatello also modelled the famous and realistic *Bust of St. Lawrence* in terracotta (on the right cabinet), which was probably the true portrait of a young Florentine boy. In the little room on the left of the apse is a magnificent *lavabo* with an *eagle* with spread wings.

In the center of the Sacristy, a large marble table which covers the *sarcophagus* of *Giovanni dei Medici and his wife Piccarda*, parents of Cosimo the Elder, by Andrea Cavalcanti (1434) Near the exit is a splendid porphyry *Sarcophagus* with bronze decorations and an exquisite marble cornice, surmounted by ample bronze tracery that divides the wall and enriches the *Tomb of Giovanni and Piero dei Medici* (sons of Cosimo the Elder), by Verrocchio (1472).

Returning to the church, on the right (no. 1 in the plan), is the

PLAN OF THE CHURCH OF S. LAURENCE AND OF THE MEDICEAN CHAPELS

A. Old Sacristy (Brunelleschi)

B. Entry to the Cloister

C. Cloister of Brunelleschi where, at the bottom, on the right, there is the staircase leading to the famous Laurenziana Library of Michelangelo.

D. Madonna Square from where, on the left, one enters the Medicean Chapels.

E. New Sacristy (Michelangelo)

1. Martelli Chapel
2-3. Pulpits by Donatello

Fig. 87 - Laurentian Library - Michelangelo: Triple Staircase of the Vestibule

Fig. 88 - Brunelleschi: Cloister of the Church of San Lorenzo

Martelli Chapel: on the altar is an *Annunciation* by Fra Filippo Lippi. Against the right wall, monument to Donatello by Romanelli (1896). On the left wall, *Sarcophagus of the Martelli Family.* Opening the door on the façade, we enter the beautiful *Cloister* in the style of Brunelleschi (fig. 88). In the corner is the statue of *Paolo Stovio* by Francesco da Sangallo. The brief staircase leads to the first floor with its splendid portico and Florentine roof. By walking around the entire portico we can better admire the vast architectural complex of San Lorenzo. To the right of the square is the entrance to the famous

Laurentian Library, open (save changes) weekdays from 10 to 13 hours. Free entrance. It is closed on holidays. When the church is closed one can get to it from the door on the left side of the church. The Library contains valuable works collected by Cosimo the Elder and Lorenzo the Magnificent, for which Pope Clement VII wanted to build a worthy seat thus commissioning Michelangelo (1524) to erect this famous Library.

Vestibule. One of this great artist's most original creations, in which the architectural planes are animated with dramatic dynamism, with double columns enclosing the limited walls, which in turn are deeply excavated by the wide windows. The TRIPLE STAIRCASE (fig. 87), designed by the Master, was finished by Vasari in 1558.

Library (fig. 87). It is daring and austere in its extremely regular form: it is, in fact, a large rectangle. In the double rows of stalls are rare and notable *Latin and Greek* manuscripts of the VI to the XVI centuries. Among the most famous documents are the celebrated *Pandects* and the V cent. *Virgil.* The beautiful floor is by Tribolo, following Michelangelo's design. The beautiful two-colored windows are by Giovanni da Udine.

Returning to Piazza San Lorenzo, to the left of the Church, walking along the animated Via dell'Ariento with its numerous stalls, ahead we can see the central Market, by Mengoni (1847), that will be remodernized soon.
As shown on the map, continuing on the left of the Canto dei Nelli, we reach Piazza Madonna where, on the left, is the entrance to the famous.

MEDICI CHAPELS

Hours (subject to changes): Summer 9:00 AM to 5:00 PM; Winter 9:00 AM to 4:00 PM. Admission L. 170
Sundays, 9:30 AM to 12:30 PM. Admission free.

From the entrance vestibule we immediately enter the vast *Medici Crypt*. The numerous inscriptions on the tombs indicate the burial place of the *Grand Dukes and members of the Medici family. Cosimo I his wife Eleanor of Toledo and their children* are buried in the first vault on the right. His father, *Giovanni dalle Bande Nere*, a great soldier, is buried near the center; the last Medici, Anna Maria Ludovica, died in 1743, is buried near the last pilaster at the right end. (In the end vault, some members of the Lorraines, successors to the Medici, are buried). The staircase leads to the grand

Capel of the Princes (fig. 89). It was begun by Nigetti (1604) on a design by Don Giovanni dei Medici, natural son of Cosimo I. It was commissioned by the Grand Duke Ferdinand I Medici who wanted to glorify his House this "Chapel" (left incomplete). It is a vast octagon with a cupola (height 52 meters), with the walls encrusted with rare marble and semiprecious stones. The *Cupola*, that originally was supposed to be made of lapislazuli, was later frescoed by Pietro Benvenuti (1829) with stories of the *Creation* and the *Final Judgement* The six sarcophagi are dedicated to the Grand Dukes buried below in the crypt. Only two niches have colossal gilded bronze statues by Pietro Tacca (XVII cent.). The other niches remained incomplete. Around the walls, on the base, are represented the sixteen coats-of-arms of Florence and other Tuscan cities (figs. 90-91). The altar and floor are modern. Behind the altar are two small rooms with precious and rare reliquaries.
Returning to the entrance, the small corridor leads to the

New Sacristy, begun by Michelangelo in 1520. It was commissioned

Fig. 89 - Chapel of the Medici Princess (San Lorenzo)
Figs. 90-91 - Coats of arms of Florence and Pisa (mosaics)

107

Fig. 92 - Michelangelo: Night (Monument to Giuliano Medici)

by the Popes Leo X and Clement VII, to hold the remains of their fathers, Lorenzo the Magnificent and Giuliano (assassinated in the Pazzi conspiracy), and other members of the Medici family. Michelangelo worked on it in periods until 1537. With the fall of the Republic, Michelangelo goes to Rome where he dies in 1564. (His body was brought to Florence and buried in St. Croce). The Capel, continued by Vasari, was left incomplete. The highly suggestive effect of the construction is due to the cupola placed on a square base, that develops Brunelleschi's themes, with its grey stone ribs against white walls, reinforced by marble structures at the base. Entering, on the left: Tomb of Lorenzo, Duke of Urbino (fig. 94) (see geneological tree), called the *Thinker*, because he is represented in profound meditation. The statues on the sarcophagus represent: *Dusk* and *Dawn*, who, in their unfinished state, are highly plastic and dramatic and suggest profound lyricism. Also buried in this tomb is his son Duke Alessandro, brother of Catherine dei Medici, last of the branch of Cosimo the Elder, assassinated by his cousin Lorenzino (1537).

Against the right wall, *Tomb of Giuliano, Duke of Nemours* (1487-1516), son of Lorenzo the Magnificent (fig. 95), idealized as a noble and strong general. The statues on the tomb: *Day* (incomplete) who is still wrapped in matter and fights to free himself (fig. 96). On

Fig. 93 - Michelangelo: Madonna and Child

the left is the famous *Night* (fig. 92), female figure, plastic and con-
tracted in the immobility of the "after-life"; at the end of human
life, restless and tormented as was his own life.

Against the entrance wall, incomplete *tomb* of Lorenzo the Magnificent and his brother Giuliano, buried below, as the inscription
reads. By Michelangelo is the *Madonna and Child* (fig. 93), sculptural
group with complex "contrapposto" movements. The two lateral
statues of *SS. Cosmos and Damian*, patrons of the Medici, are by
followers of Michelangelo, Angelo Montorsoli and Raffaello da
Montelupo.

Figs. 94-95 - Michelangelo: Monuments to Lorenzo and Giuliano Medici

Returning to San Lorenzo Square, farther ahead, the short Via dei Gori (on the
side of the Medici Palace) leads to the small Square of St. Giovannino degli
Scolopi.

On the right, observe the beautiful *Façade* of the church of the same name that
Ammannati built with his own money. The artist is buried in the interior of
the church, to the left of the entrance, as remembered by the inscription. With
this Square, Via Martelli end and Via Cavour begins (at one time called Via
Larga), where we admire the palace called Medici-Riccardi Palace.

Fig. 96 - Michelangelo: Day (Monument to Giuliano Medici)

MEDICI-RICCARDI PALACE

Hours (subject to changes): week-days 9:00 AM to 1:00 PM; 3:00 PM to 5:30 PM. Admission L. 100. Sundays: 9-12:00. Free entrance.

This splendid Renaissance palace (fig. 97) typical example of a wealthy person home, was built by Michelozzo (1440-60) on order of Cosimo the Elder. The *façade*, elegant and majestic with its stories of graduated rustic ashlar, terminates on high with the splendid and classic cornice. The beautiful mullioned windows, became examples for "Renaissance" architecture. Among the people who lived here were Cosimo the Elder, Lorenzo the Magnificent and his successors, among whom was Catherine dei Medici, the future Queen of France. Among the foreign Sovereigns were: Charles VIII of France and Charles V of Spain. In 1655 the Medici moved their home to the Pitti Palace and sold this palace to the Riccardi family, who enlarged it by seven windows per story and included the entrance to the stables, on Via Larga (today Via Cavour). Similar additions were made on the side facing Via Ginori. Later the Palace passed over to the State and became the seat of the Prefecture.

Courtyard, with an arcade, and the upper Loggia closed with windows. The beautiful *medallions* in the architrave are attributed to Bertoldo, pupil of Donatello, and the *graffiti* are by Maso di Bartolomeo (1452). While the *first floor* has elegant double arched

111

Fig. 97 - Medici - Riccardi Palace

windows, the *second floor* presents an elegant "ionic collonade". Unfortunately the courtyard is overpowered by the decorations added by the Riccardi family, which should be removed. The statue of Orpheus is by Bandinelli. On the left the

Medici Museum is laid out in the first four rooms where Lorenzo the Magnificent had his appartments. Together with the important collection of documents of the Medici family and collateral branches, are displayed works by Granacci, Bronzino, portrait painter of the Medici court, and Filippo Lippi with his famous *Madonna and Child*, rendered with profound humanity. Through the glass door on the right, we climb to the

Chapel of Benozzo Gozzoli, pupil of Fra Angelico (1459-60), painter of a pleasant narrative vein who, in these celebrated frescoes, glorified the Medici, against a background of the outskirts of Florence and the green Tuscan countryside. Since the Chapel has no windows, the artist had to overcome this difficulty with the aid of artificial light. Entering, on the right wall we admire, the *Procession of the Wise Kings* (fig. 98) against the background of the luminous, steep hill of Vincigliata, between Fiesole and Settignano. Under the Oriental features and clothes of the Kings and their following, we can recognize Greek and Florentine personalities of the XV cent., who participated in the famous parade that was held on the occasion of the Council of 1439. It is believed that the artist was also inspired by the tournament of 1459 for the visit of Pius II, which saw the Medici in all their fast and splendor. The first young horseman is supposed to be Lorenzo the Magnificent, idealized, with his gracious sisters Bianca Maria and Nannina. Among the people in the following, we recognize, Piero Medici, among the first on high, and in the corner, a *self portrait* of the artist, with his name on his hat. On the following wall: *John VII Emperor of Byzantium*. Followed on the other wall by *Joseph, Patriarch of Costantinople*, riding the mule, who died during the Council and was buried in St. Maria Novella. In the handsome young man, riding with a leopard, it is believed that the artist idealized *Giuliano*, the brother of Lorenzo the Magnificent. The splendid *ceiling*, the *stalls and the polychrome marble floors* were executed following designs by Michelozzo. On the altar a *Madonna and Child*, copy by Neri di Bicci from an original by Fra Filippo Lippi, at one time on display here, now at the Berlin Museum. On the small walls of the altar, we can admire Gozzoli's *musical Angels*, against the beautiful Tuscan countryside where the Medici had their villas. Returning to the courtyard, the staircase on the right leads to the FIRST FLOOR, in the splendid rooms of the Prefecture. On the left and then to the right, we enter the famous *Room* of *Luca Giordano* (1682-83) where the artist of the same name frescoed the vault with the *Apotheosis of Cosimo III* with perspec-

Fig. 98 - Medici - Riccardi Palace (Chapel) - Benozzo Gozzoli: Procession of the Wise Kings

tive effects. The *Room*, enriched with gilded mirrors, benches and seats, is now reserved for the Provincial Council that holds its reunions here.

Returning to Via Cavour, farther ahead on the left, we arrive at San Marco Square.

SAN MARCO SQUARE (see city plan n. 7)

In the center of the square (fig. 99) is a mediocre bronze monument of General Manfredo Fanti by Pio Fedi (1873).

CHURCH OF SAN MARCO

The original XII century construction was modified by Michelozzo and Silvani. The façade is Baroque and is by Giovacchino Pronti (1780).

Interior has a single nave. In the center of the great carved ceiling is a *Madonna in Glory* by Pucci (XVIII cent.). Above the entrance is a large *Crucifix* from the Giottesque school. Among the other works we remember: on the second altar of the right wall, *Madonna* *and Saints* by Fra Bartolommeo (1509); on the third altar, *large mosaic* of the VIII cent. representing the *Virgin Praying* (originally in the Oratory of Pope John VII in Rome). The next altar was inserted in the arch by Giambologna (1580), over which there is a statue of St. Zenobius, by the same artist.

Main Chapel by Silvani with frescoes representing the *Glory of the Dominican Order*, by Gherardini (1717): the *Last Supper* is of the Florentine school of the XVIII cent.; on the walls, *the Wedding of Cana* and the *Epiphany* frescoed by the French artist Parrocel (1702); on the left of the Main Chapel is the *Serragli Chapel* or of the "Sacrament", decorated with late XVI cent. paintings. On the left wing is the *Altar of Saint Antonino*, where the embalmed body of the Saint is conserved. On the wall of the left nave are the *tombstones* of Giovanni Pico della Mirandola (1463-94) and of the humanist poet Agnolo Poliziano. Leaving the church, on the left is the entrance to San Marco Museum.

SAN MARCO MUSEUM

(Save changes it is closed Mondays. For the hours see listing at beginning of book).

The restoration of this complex was made possible by Cosimo the Elder, great banker and politician of vast foresight who greatly protected the monastic orders, aware of their influence on the people, whom he in turn tried to pro-

Fig. 99 - Square, Church and Museum of St. Mark

pitiate with every means. On his order, Michelozzo (1437-52), his favorite artist, restored the bell-tower and brought the fallen monastery back to its old splendor, having been left vacant by the suppressed Salvestrine friars. Beato Angelico (Guido Guidolino di Pietro), borno in Vicchio di Mugello 1387, who, at the age of twenty, became a friar in the Convent of San Domenico, transferred here with his fellow priests. He acquired his art from Lorenzo Monaco and the miniaturists that flourished in Florence. Later he turned his attention to the new pictorial vision of Masaccio, and combined the compactness of the forms to his delicate color. Having become famous for his frescoes in Orvieto and the Vatican, in 1449 he was named Prior of San Marco and in 1452 of San Domenico where, as a young man, with his brother Benedetto, manuscript writer, he had renounced the pleasures of the world. He died in Rome in 1445 and was buried in St. Maria della Minerva. For his mild personality and his mystical art he was given the name Beato Angelico. In this monastery also lived Friar Antonio Pierozzi (1389-1445), acclaimed bishop of Florence, later sanctified. Cosimo the Elder, appreciated his discussions and often left the palace and retired here where he had his private cell. Savonarola was called from Ferrara by Lorenzo the Magnificent and became Prior, and Bartolommeo della Porta, Renaissance painter and fervent follower of Savonarola's, entered the Dominican order. The Convent passed to the State in 1860. After 1920, with material collected from other sources, the Museum was constituted, entirely dedicated to B. Angelico.

First Cloister (fig. 100). A splendid example of Renaissance monastic architecture, shaded by flower-beds and the beautiful cedar of Lebanon. This first cloister is called "of St. Antonino" because of the XVI century frescoes, with episodes of the life of the bishop-saint. At the end of the portico, in front of the entrance, *St. Domenic at the Foot of the Crucifix* by Angelico.

Moving to the right, in a lunette, *St. Antonino acclaimed Bishop enters the Cathedral*, that we see with the original façade destroyed in 1588, frescoed by Poccetti. In the lunette at the end, *Comiso the elder orders Michelozzo and Helpers to rebuild the Convent.* In the lunette on the right, *Jesus dressed as a Pilgrim received by two Dominicans*, by Angelico. On the right:

Old Hospice of the Pilgrims. A large rectangular room, divided into sections, where Angelico's works have been displayed. The splendid collection crearly shows the evolution of the artist, who goes from the light and abstract tones of Lorenzo Monaco, and arrives at the Renaissance vision (*Madonna of the Linaioli*, cited ahead), in which he reaches great effects of devotion. Against the long right wall: table with *Madonna and Child with Saints*. In the panels: scenes from the *lives of SS. Cosmos and Damian*; the one about the *Burial* shows St. Mark's Square with the old Convent. Against the long left wall we can admire the panels, which once formed the doors of a tabernacle containing silver in the Sacristy of SS. Annunziata, with *Episodes in the life of the Virgin and Christ*, divided into 35 small scenes painted by Angelico and helpers, among whom Baldo-

Fig. 100 - St. Mark - First Cloister

vinetti. Among the most interesting, observe the *Flight into Egypt.*
Farther ahead, on the back of the second divider: *Final Judgement*
(restored), where, among the Elect, Angelico glorified the Dominican
order (fig. 101), while, among the Damned (work of helpers), are
represented unworthy monks and prelates. In the other section:
large *Deposition* (c. 1440, restored). On the back of the divider are:
the famous, delicate *Madonna of the Star* (c. 1430); and the exquisite
Annunciation with, below, *Adoration of the Magi* that reveals Angelico as a fine miniaturist. In the opposite section, among the episodes of the Virgin rendered with intense religiousness, are *Scenes
of Zacharius writing the name of the infant John,* while in the background opens an admirable view of a Tuscan villa.
On the wall at the far end, large *Deposition* (c. 1435), rendered
with intense humanity and a strong religious feeling. In the *Joseph
of Arimathea, with the black cap, holding the body of Christ,* he
portrayed Michelozzo, the architect of the convent. In the pinnacles:
Noli me tangere, Ressurection, the Marys at the Sepulchre by Lorenzo Monaco, teacher of Angelico. Returning to the entrance wall,
we admire the famous and large *Madonna of the Flax Workers,*
expressed by Angelico in full Renaissance forms, inside the beautiful
frame by Ghiberti. In the leaves, *St. John the Baptist* and *St. Mark
the Apostle;* in the predella *the preaching of St. Peter, Adoration of*

Fig. 101 · Fra' Angelico · Final Judgement (detail)

the Magi and *the Martyrdom of St. Mark.* Returning in the cloister at the end of the cloister, to the right,

Lavatory. Dedicated to Fra Bartolomeo, Renaissance painter active in this convent (1472-1517), by whom admire here some minor works and the majestic, incomplete *Madonna and Child*, with Leonardesque type shading.
On the right (if open),

Old Refectory of the Salvestrines. On the right wall is a large fresco, deteriorated with time, by Fra Bartolomeo and Albertinelli, representing the *Final Judgement.* Ahead is a Baroque pulpit. On the end wall, fresco by Sogliani (XVI cent.) of the *Crucifixion*, and below, *Episodes of St. Dominic* who, left without provisions, prays with his friars and receives aid from the Angels; on the sides *St. Anthony and St. Catherine of Siena.* Coming back to the cloister, ahead and to the right is the

Chapter Room where we can admire the large *Crucifixion* and below, *the Madonna and the Holy Women among the Saints and Founders of the Monastic orders,* a masterpiece of Angelico's painting (1442). Under the portico is the famous bell called "la piagnona" (the crier) attributed to Donatello, that, at the time of Savonarola, was in the bell-tower of the Church. It is the historic bell that called everyone to prayer on the tragic day that St. Mark's was put under seige for the arrest of Savonarola, who was called "il piagnone", because he lamented the misfortunes of the citizens due to the corrupt times, prophesizing what would come about if the city was not rid of the evil that was undermining her.

Farther ahead to the right we enter the small *Corridor* that leads to the second cloister by Michelozzo (closed to the public because it is the property of the monks). Through the glass door we can observe this *second cloister* and the modern rooms of the first floor where the Dominican friars live. Guido Carocci collected, in this cloister, many architectural fragments originally in the old center of the city. The beautiful staircase on the right leads to the

First Floor. From the beautiful ceiling to the small cells, it is conserved in its original structure, that reminds us of the times and the stark living quarters of famous Dominicans. On the wall at the head of the stairs, the famous *Annunciation* by Beato Angelico (fig. 102), against a Renaissance portico background. Moving along the left corridor, we point out that the frescoes in the cells on the right are by followers of Angelico, while those on the left are, for the most part, by the master himself. They represent; in the first cell, *Noli me tangere*; third cell, *Annunciation* of a light and simple composition; sixth cell, *Transfiguration*; ninth cell, *Incoronation*. Walking down the entire length of the corridor, at the end, on the right, we enter the

Prior's Quarter. Consists of a vestibule and two small cells and was where Savonarola lived. In the vestibule are two pantings by Fra Bartolomeo representing: *Portrait of Savonarola* and *St. Peter Martyr* in the semblance of Savonarola. The *execution of Savonarola in Signoria Square* is a copy from an old print. The small marble monument by Duprè (1873) shows *Savonarola before the Magistrates.* The study room contains, remains of a tunic, a rosary and other objects belonging to Savonarola. In the bedroom, *Crucifix* in the style of Angelico that, it is believed, Savonarola used when he preached in the Florentine squares after his excomunication. The rooms, severe and suggestive, bring to mind Florence divided into "piagnoni" and "arrabbiati" (criers and the angry), and Savonarola's personality, still much discussed. Walking toward the exit, the left hand cells have frescoes of *St. Dominic at the foot of the Cross* by Angelico's helpers.

On the wall halfway down the corridor: *Madonna and Saints* by Angelico and helpers. Returning to the entrance, observe on the right wall, the *Crucifix* with *St. Dominic praying* by Angelico. Continuing on the left, cell no. 31 (at the head of the stairs) where St.

Fig. 102 - St. Mark's Museum - Angelico: Annunciation

Antonino lived, containing the *geneological tree of the Dominicans, death mask*, and other sacred objects belonging to the Saint.

Following is the double cell no. 32 where Angelico is said to have lived, later altered, with frescoes attributed to the master. Farther ahead, from the large window, a splendid view of the courtyard. Among the frescoes that can be admired in the small cells that follow are: in cell no. 34, *Prayer in the Garden*; in cell no. 35, the *Communion of the Apostles in the presence of the Virgin* by Angelico. On the right of the corridor, cells 38 and 39 were reserved for Cosimo the Elder, when he would leave his palace and retire here to meditate. In the first, that served as a vestibule, *Crucifixion* from the school of Gozzoli; in the second, *bust of St. Antonino, portrait of Cosimo the Elder* and, on the front wall, the *Epiphany*, with the personages thought to be those seen by Angelico during the Council of Florence of 1439 which took place under Cosimo's patronage. Returning toward the exit, on the left, opposite to the large window, we enter the splendid

Library. Vast rectangular room, divided into three naves by small, slim columns (1441), where Michelozzo created the prototype of the Renaissance library, but at the same time stayed within the range of the monastic tradition. In the cases are valuable liturgical manuscripts of the XIV and XV centuries. At the entrance of the library, we observe on the wall, the epigraph that commemorates the place where Savonarola was arrested on April 8, 1498.

Heading toward the exit, at the bottom of the stairs, on the right is the

Small Refectory, where Domenico Ghirlandaio (c. 1483) frescoed the *Last Supper* that he repeated, with variations, in the Convent of Ognissanti. On the walls, valuable "Della Robbias".

Leaving the Museum and looking at the large wall on Via Cavour, that encloses the garden (today belonging to the Officers' Club) we see the plaque that marks the place where the "Old Accademy of St. Mark" was held, in which Michelangelo, in contrast with his father's wishes made his first passes in sculpture, encouraged and helped by Lorenzo the Magnificent. At the end of the wall on the right is the imposing construction by Buontalenti (1574), called "Casino of St. Mark", now the Court of Appeals. On the right of the Museum, on Via Lamarmora, is the Administration Building of the University of Florence. At the beginning of Via Ricasoli is the graceful Loggia of the XIV cent., restored in 1935, that was once a part of the old hospital of S. Matteo, now seat of the Accademy of Fine Arts. Farther ahead, at no. 60 Via Ricasoli, is the entrance to the Gallery of the Accademy and Tribune of David.

Fig. 103 - Gallery of the Accademy and Tribune of David

GALLERY OF THE ACCADEMY AND TRIBUNE OF DAVID

(Save changes, it is closed Mondays)

From the vestibule we enter the large room (fig. 103) where we can admire the *Prisoners* which leads us triumphantly up to the celebrated David (fig. 104) by Michelangelo (height of the statue 5,10 meters, base 2 meters). It was sculpted by the artist between 1501 and 1505, when he was about 25 years old. It is a symbolic statue which had been placed in front of the Signoria Palace, as the guardian of liberty of the Florentine Republic, and moved here in 1873, having been replaced in Signoria Square by a copy. The heroic figure of a young athlete, sculpted during one of Michelangelo's most serene moments, is shown in the act of vigil expectation, his body showing vibrant tension, determined to win or die. On the stand to the right of the David, *bronze bust of Michelangelo*, by his pupil and friend Daniele da Volterra. On the walls of the Gallery are splendid and priceless Flemish tapestries with *Stories from Genesis*, following cartoons by the Flemish painter Van Orley (1552). Below, we can admire the celebrated *Prisoners* who seem to fight with the material that envelops them in order to emerge plastically. These famous statues were conceived for the tomb of Pope Julius II, but were made smaller than originally planned.

Between these Prisoners on the right, is the *St. Matthew*, a statue destined for the Cathedral together with a series of Apostles. In this incomplete work, Michelangelo surpasses classical art, showing, with great vigor, his phylosophical and dramatic concept of the "idea enclosed in the marble", to be liberated "little by little". Farther ahead, on the right is a *Pietà* called *Palestrina Pietà* because it came from Palestrina near Rome, when it was given to the Gallery by the State in 1940 (fig. 105). Some critics believe it to be by his followers since it does not have the dramatic force as found in the "Pietà" in the Cathedral.

At the end of the left wing of the Tribune are two original plaster models by Giambologna for his marble statues of: the *Rape of the Sabines* (in Signoria Square), and the *Virtue that defeats Vice* (in the Bargello). To the left we enter

Rooms I, II, III that contain paintings historically selected from the XIII and XIV centuries; among the most notable, the *Magdalen* by the "Master of the Maddalena", the *Pietà* by Giovanni da Milano (1365) and the *Stories of St. Francis and Christ*, by Taddeo Gaddi. When the remodelling works are completed in the old *Room IV*, with the splendid ceiling, paintings of the XV and XVI centuries will be displayed. Among the most important works we point out that of Lorenzo Monaco and the rare *scene of a Saint in a hospital*, by

Fig. 104 - Michelangelo: David

124

Fig. 105 - Michelangelo: Palestrina Pietà

Pontormo, remembering the ward of the old hospital of S. Matteo, that was here at one time. Heading toward the exit, after Michelangelo's Pietà, on the left we enter the remodelled rooms, in which, at the entrance we can admire the famous *Cassone* or marriage chest, by an unknown Florentine of the XV cent., improperly called the *Wedding Procession of the Adimari* (fig. 106), interesting for its artistic value and for its portraits of Florentines shown in the typical

Fig. 106 - Unknown Florentine: Adimari Wedding Procession (detail)

costumes and hairdos of the era, in S. Giovanni Square. In the successive rooms, among the most important works: graceful *Madonna and Child* attributed to Botticelli. Also shown are other works by Florentine artists and by Perugino.

Leaving the Gallery and turning to the left we arrive at the nearby Square of the Belle Arti where, at no. 80 Via degli Alfani (from 10:00 to 12:00 hours), you can visit the small but important Museum of musical instruments of the **Luigi Cherubini conservatory.**

Farther ahead, at no. 78, entrance to the

Museum of Pietre dure or Mosaics the only one of its kind, begun by Duke Ferdinand I Medici (1588). This "factory" that enriched the Chapel of the Princes in St. Lorenzo with its rare stones originating from all parts of the world, furnishes material of an elevated decorative value to churches, palaces and Museums in Florence, Italy and the world.

THIRD ITINERARY

Piazza della Repubblica - Straw Market - Via por Santa Maria - Ponte Vecchio - Pitti Palace: Palatine Gallery, Royal Appartments, Museum of Silverware, Boboli Gardens, Gallery of Modern Art, Museum of Antique Coaches - Church of S. Spirito - Church of the Carmine.
This itinerary is indicated by numbers 11, 12, 13, 14, 15 and 16 on our monumental map)

PIAZZA DELLA REPUBBLICA (Republic Square)

Formerly Piazza Vittorio Emanuele II. In order to build this square the Old Market, economic hearth of Old Florence (1895), was destroyed, as can be read above the large, overpowering arch. On the left is the portico of the Central Post Office, by Sabatini and Vagnetti (1917). This Square is a popular meeting place for Florentines and turists because of its many cafès.

In front of the hotel Savoy, on a tall column, is a reproduction of the statue of *Abundance*, that was found here at the time of the "Old Market". To the right of the "Upim" department store, the short and elegant Via Calimala leads to the well known *Straw Market* (new market) with the Loggia by Giovanni Battista del Tasso (1547-51). The famous "wild boar" (fig. 107), called "il Porcellino" (the little pig), by Tacca (1612, restored), is a copy of a classical marble statue currently in the Uffizi Gallery. At one time the Banking Center, (mentioned in the introduction) was found here. In the center of the Loggia is a small round slab, upon which the bankrupts were effectively punished. Por Santa Maria (with its buildings reconstructed from the ruins of the last war) partly conserves its medieval character because of a few "Tower-houses" especially those on Via delle Terme and Borgo SS. Apostoli, on the right. On the left, the *Square and the Church of SS. Stefano and Cecilia*, originally built in 1116, worked over later, and, having been destroyed in 1944 by German mines, has been restored to its original aspect.

Farther ahead the Ponte Vecchio.

Ponte Vecchio (fig. 108), attributed to Neri di Fioravanti (1348), who replaced an old wooden bridge destroyed by the flood of 1333 it was damaged in 1944 by the retreatig Germans and by the flood of Nov. 4, 1966). The Ponte Vecchio (Old Bridge), with its small characteristic shops, is known throughout the world as the jewellers' bridge; formerly there were butcher shops. On the terrace is a square based monument surmounted by a bust of *Cellini* by Romanelli

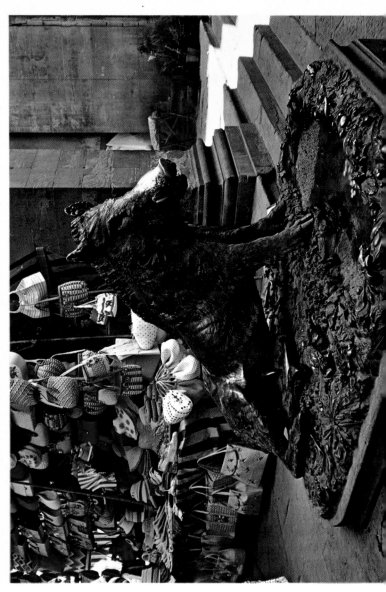

Fig. 107 - Loggia of the Mercato Nuovo - The Wild Boar by Tacca

g. 108 · Ponte Vecchio (Old Bridge)

900). Above the shops, on the left hand side, is the "Vasarian
rridor" that joins the Uffizi Gallery to the Pitti Palace. After the
onte Vecchio begins Via Guicciardini, rebuilt after the war. Farther
ead to the left, under the Vasarian corridor, is the *Square* and
urch of S. Felicita (XI cent.), erected on an old cemetery, worked
er in the successive centuries. Under the portico of the Church,
the right, among other works, is the *Tomb of Cardinal de' Rossi*
Raffaelle da Montelupo, brought here in 1736. In the interior
e can admire the famous *Deposition* by Pontormo, in the first
apel on the right. The Capponi Chapel that Brunelleschi built for
e Barbadori family was later altered by Ruggeri during the remo-
lling of the church. The balcony on high was used by the Grand
ukes of Lorraine when they came here from the Pitti Palace for
eir religious services. Continuing along Via Guicciardini, at no. 18
a plaque marking the house in which Machiavelli lived. Ahead
the left is the *Guicciardini Palace* with its beautiful garden, at-
ibuted to Baccio d'Agnolo. Here the historian Guicciardini was
orn.
e therefore reach the vast square dominated by the imposing Pitti
alace.

129

Fig. 109 - Pitti Palace

PITTI PALACE

The Palace is built of ashlar (fig. 109), inspired by ancient Roma
constructions. It was begun by Luca Fancelli (1458), following
design by Brunelleschi, to satisfy the great ambitions of the influen
tial banker Luca Pitti, one time friend and follower of the Medic
who, jealous of their power, plotted against Piero the "gouty". Th
conspiracy was discovered thanks to the careful surveillance of h
young son Lorenzo (later the Magnificent).

Luca Pitti, ruined by his banking speculations, left the Palace in
complete. Later in 1540, Cosimo I (with the dowry brought by h
wife Eleanor of Toledo) bought it from Bonaccorso, Luca's grea
grandson.

Cosimo I moved here from Palazzo Vecchio and ordered Vasari t
join the two palaces with the corridor that runs over the Ponte Vec
chio. Eleanor of Toledo commissioned Tribolo to transform th
hillside called "Boboli" into the famous "Boboli Garden" tha
scenically enclose the Palace. The original building consisted of thre
doors alternated by four windows on the ground floor, seven win
dows on the upper floors and was crowned with a panoramic loggi
Ammannati, more known as an architect than as a sculptor (1558

igs. 110-111 - Valerio Cioli: Dwarf Morgante - Buontalenti: Grotto

ithout altering Brunelleschi's plan, closed two doors substituting
nem with windows, lengthened the façade and created the most
eautiful courtyard of the Renaissance on the interior. Later Giulio
nd Alfonso Parigi (1620) further lengthened the façade, adding three
indows on each side. Between 1764-1819 Giuseppe Ruggeri added
ne so-called "rondò", the beautiful lateral portico which juts out
nto the square. When the Medici died out, the Palace became the
ome of the Lorraines, who were driven out in 1859. During the
eriod when Florence was the capital of Italy (1865-71), the Palace
as host to the Savoy court. After 1871, it was the private home of
ne royal family. With the advent of the Republic (1946), the great
alace and all its art treasures, became property of the State.
)n the left of the façade, from the gate called of "Bacchus" because
f the grotesque fountain (fig. 110) by Valerio Cione, representing
Aorgante dwarf riding a tortoise, one can reach the Grotto of Buonalenti (fig. 111) and from here the Boboli Garden, mentioned later.
ee above the already said Vasari's Corridor, reopened to the public
n 1973, full of works and selfportraits of famous artists.

ROYAL APARTMENTS

1-2 Vestibule
3 Gallery of the statues
4 Dining Hall (or of the niches)
5 Green Hall
6 Hall of the Throne
7 Blue Hall
8 Chapel
9 Hall of the parrots
10 Yellow Hall
11 Sleeping room of the Queen
12 Sleeping room of the King
13 Study
14 Sitting room
15 Antechamber
16 Hall of Bona
17 Dancing Hall (or White Hall)

PITTI PALACE
PALATINA GALLERY
1st Floor

I Hall of Venus
II Hall of Apollo
III Hall of Mars
IV Hall of Jupiter
V Hall of Saturn
VI Hall of the Iliad
VII Hall of the Stove
VIII Hall of the Education
of Jupiter
Bath
IX Hall of Ulysses
X Hall of Prometheus
XI Corridor of the columns
XII Hall of the Justice

XIV Hall of Flora
XV Hall of Putti
XVI Hall of Poccetti
XVII Hall of music

XVIII Hall of Castagnoli
XIX-XXIII Quarter of Volterano
XXIV-XXVIII Halls closed to the
Public

A. Vestibule
B. Hall of the Cup
C. Terrace
D. Ammannati's Court-yard

GARDEN

BOBOLI

PITTI SQUARE

ENTRY

Fig. 112 - Palatine Gallery: Iliad Room
Figs. 113-114 - Sustermans: Portrait of Prince Waldemar of Denmark - Raphael:
Madonna of the Grand duke

PALATINE GALLERY

(Closed, save changes, every Monday. For hours see beginning of the book).

One reaches the Gallery from the main staircase of the palace, built by Ammanati on the right corner of the arcade looking on to the courtyard.

Palatine Gallery, which was begun by Cosimo II (1620). The vast collectio was continuously enriched by his successors. Because of the marriage of Anr Maria Ludovica Medici and John William, the Elector Palatine, the museu was called "Palatine Gallery". In 1820 tre museum was opened to the publ by the Lorraines (successors of the Medici), and in 1911, it was ceded to tr State by Vittorio Emanuele III. The vision that the Gallery offers is splendic especially on the days when the "Royal Appartments" are opened an tr perspective effect of these sumptuous rooms is lengthned.

Here the works of art are not placed in chronological order as in the Uffi Gallery, but rather displayed with an essentially decorative taste according to tr spirit of the princely courts. It is a picture gallery. To facilitate the visit w have included a practical plan. We mention that the works not cited can b easily identified by reading their relative plates.

Room I. Of Venus. Here ends the series of splendid rooms built for Cosimo I the initiator of this Gallery. In the vault frescoed by Pietro da Cortona an Ciro Ferri (1641-42) we see *Minerva* (wisdom), who leads away from *Venus* th idealized figure of Cosimo I (in vain held back by Eros), directing him towar Hercules. The stuccoes representing various Medici personalities, are by Roma artists. Moving from left to right, by Titian we see "*la bella*" (restored) an the *Portrait of Pietro Aretino*. Between these two paintings is the *Sacred Co: versation* by Pitati. Above, a large *Seascape* by the Neapolitan Salvator Ros who also painted the one on the opposite wall. At the beginning and at th end of the next wall are two very rare *Landscapes* by Rubens: *Return of tr Peasants from the Fields* (fig. 125) and *Ulysses on the Islands of the Faeci*. O the far wall: *Portrait of Jiulius II*, a copy by Titian of an original by Rapha (now lost). Next is the celebrated *Concert* (fig. 126), once attributed to Gio gione, now believed to be a young work by Titian.

From this room we enter the sumptuous *Royal Appartments*. These rooms ar open on alternating days with the Museum of Silverware on the ground floo that is, Thursdays, Saturdays and the first and third Sundays of the mont (subject to changes).

Room II. Of Apollo. Its name derives from the subject of the ceiling, by Pietro d Cortona and Ciro Ferri (1642-46), who decorated it with white and colored stuc coes and Medici crests. In the center of the vault, the *Glorification of Cosimo ,* shown in the figure of the *young man*, whom *Virtue* and *Glory* lead to *Apoll* in the presence of Hercules, Nymphs and Atlantis. On the wall near the wir dow is the famous and exuberant *Mary Magdalen* (fig. 123), a typical femal representation by Titian with its warm and golden color. Also by Titian w can admire, on the right of the door, the celebrated *Portrait of the Gentlema with the Grey Eyes*, considered one of the most important portraits by Titia and Italian art. Above is the ample *Deposition* by Andrea del Sarto. On th following walls: *Madonna and Saints*, by Rosso Fiorentino, one of the majc works of this mannerist painter whose figures are tormented and whose color i vivid and fiery; *Holy Family* by Andrea Del Sarto, rendered with classical equ librium; *Cleopatra* by Guido Reni, placed here temporarily. On the wall nea the window: *Portraits of Charles I of England and Henriette of France*, daughte

Fig. 115 - Room of Saturn - Raphael: Madonna of the Chair

Figs. 116-117 - Raphael: Portraits of Angelo and Maddalena Doni
Fig. 118 - Palatine Gallery - Room of Jupiter

f Maria dei Medici (restored work, believed by some to be of Van Dyck's
chool).

Room III. Of Mars. On the ceiling, Allegory of Mars by Pietro da Cortona and
Ciro Ferri (1645-47). Moving from left to right, two beautiful *Madonnas and
Child*, by Murillo (fig. 121). Between these two, *the Four Philosophers*, by
Rubens (fig. 122), who portrayed himself in the figure standing on the left.
Seated next to him is his *brother Philip*, humanist and philosopher, followed
by the distinguished philosopher Justus Lipsius, who seems to be explaining
passage from Seneca, and his pupil Jan Wouver (restored work). Followed
by a *Portrait of a Man* by Veronese and the large *Consequences of War*, by
Rubens (1638), alluding to the thirty-year war that devastated a great part of
Europe. Next is Titian's *Portrait of Cardinal Ippolito dei Medici* in a Hungarian
costume. Next is the famous *Portrait of Cardinal Bentivoglio* by Van Dick from
Antwerp (1559-1640), a deeply psychological interpretation rendered with elegance and simplicity. Finally, by Tintoretto, *Portrait of Luigi Cornaro*, author.

Room IV. Of Jupiter (fig. 118). The ceiling by Pietro da Cortona and Ciro Ferri
1643-46) representing the *Allegory of Jupiter* with reference to the glories of
Cosimo I. In the center of the room is the awkward and mediocre *Victory* by
Consano (1867), that should be removed in order to allow us to admire the
many important works of art. From left to right: *young St. John the Baptist*
restored) by Andrea del Sarto (fig. 119). Followed by the *Deposition* by Fra'
Bartolomeo, with its pyramidal composition. Above, *Nymphs attacked by the
Satyrs* by Rubens. Followed by the *Portrait of Guidobaldo della Rovere*, by
Bronzino, and the grandiose figure of *St. Mark* by Fra' Bartolomeo, who was
inspired by Michelangelo's prophets. Above the door, the *Annunciation* by Andrea del Sarto and the *Assumption*, left incomplete because of the artist's death.
On the next wall, *Battle Scene* by the French artist Jacques Courtois, called il
Borgognone. Near the door is the famous *Fornarina* (baker's daughter) by Raphael (fig. 120), magnificent portrait rendered with the warmth of Venetian
color, known as *the Veiled Lady*. The beautiful Roman brunette is the same
one that the artist idealized in the Madonna of the Chair. Near the window:
Three Ages of Man, school of Giorgione of the early XVI cent. On the apposite
wall, *Madonna del Sacco* by Perugino (restored). Against the walls are valuable
tables made with Florentine mosaics.

Room V. Of Saturn with the ceiling representing the *Allegory of Saturn*, alluding
to the virtues of Cosimo I, frescoed by Pietro da Cortona and Ciro Ferri (1663-
665). This room contains a great number of works by Raphael. Beginning from
left to right we can admire: the *Madonna of the Grand Duke* (1504) by Raphael, so called because it was the favorite of the Medici Grand Dukes, inspired
by Perugino and Leonardo's "sfumato". Following are the *St. Peter* by Guer-
cino and the realistic *Portrait of a man* by Carracci. Above, the *Dispute of the
Holy Trinity* by Andrea del Sarto (1517), that inspired Raphael for the same
subject in the Vatican. Below is the *Portrait of Tommaso Inghirami*, by Raphael
c. 1514). Following, by the same artist are: the famous *Portraits of Angelo and
Maddalena Doni* (1506 - figs. 116-117). Between these two is the *Vision of
Ezechiel* (c. 1518), showing the influence of Michelangelo. Above, *Madonna of
the Baldaquin* (1506), incomplete. Next, by Perugino are the large *Deposition*,
with its beautiful Umbrian landscape, and the exquisite *Mary Magdalen*, below.
The solemn and monumental *Jesus and the Evangelists*, above right, is by Fra'

Figs. 119-120 - Room of Jupiter - A. Del Sarto: St. John - Raphael: the Veiled Lady

Figs. 121-122 - Room of Mars - Murillo: Madonna and Child - Rubens: Four Philisophers

Bartolomeo. Below, *Portrait of an Unknown Man*, called the *Goldsmith* is attributed to Ridolfo del Ghirlandaio. On the following wall are: Portrait of Cardinal Dovizzi da Bibbiena, believed to be by Raphael's helpers: *St. Rose* and the graceful *St. John Sleeping* by Dolci; and finally, the famous *Madonna of the Chair* (fig. 115) by Raphael, painted in Rome (1515-16) using his beloved "Fornarina" as a model.

Room VI. Iliad Room (fig. 112). This rooms was added by the Dukes of Lorraine. In the ceiling, frescoed by Luigi Sabatelli (1819), are *Episodes* taken from the Homeric poem. In the center of the room is the statue of *Charity* by Lorenzo Bartolini (1824), rendered with profound humanity. Beginning at the left and moving toward the right: *Portrait of an unknown woman*, called *The Pregnant Lady* (Gravida) by Raphael (c. 1505), from his Florentine period. Next is the grandiose *Assumption* by Andrea del Sarto, who repeats the same subject in the large picture on the opposite wall. Ahead is a *Portrait of a Woman* by Ridolfo del Ghirlandaio (son of Domenico), who was inspired by Raphael's *Gravida*.

On the following wall, among the numerous works, we mention the large canvas showing the *extasy of St. Philip Neri* by Maratta (XVIII cent.) of the Roman school, inspired by Guido Reni.

Near the windows, famous *Portrait of Waldemar Christian*, Prince of Denmark, by Sustermans (fig. 113) and the rare *Equestrian Portrait of Philip IV of Spain*, by Velasquez (restored).

ROYAL APPARTMENTS

Remodelled in Empire style by the Savoy family, these rooms witnessed the most famous court receptions. (The royal family's private life evolved in the small adjoining nineteenth century palace called "La Meridiana", built by the Dukes of Lorraine, with its entrance from the Boboli Garden behind Ammannati's courtyard, joined to the "large Palace" by an internal passageway). Among the most important works in these sumptuous ex-royal Appartments we mention:

Room 4. Of the Niches (Dining Room). So-called because of the copies of classical statues in the niches of a purely decorative value. The neo-classic decoration is by Giuseppe Maria Terreni and Giuseppe Castagnoli. On the walls is a series of portraits of the Medici in their different costumes, by Sustermans, the court painter of the Medici family. Also seen here are Japanese and Sevres vases. The large rectangular table is covered with a precious embroidered tapestry of the XVIII cent.

Room 5. Green Room (formerly room of the guard). Called Green room for the color of the brocade that covers the walls. The decoration is by Castagnoli while the chiaroscuro ceiling, with allegorical

Figs. 123-124 - Room of Apollo - Titian: Mary Magdalen and the Gentleman with the grey eyes

subjects in honor of the Medici, is by Luca Giordano. On the walls are four Gobelins tapestries with *stories of Esther*, made by Audran following cartoons by Jean François de Troy (1737-40). The large intarsia cabinet is of XVII cent.

Room 6. Throne Room (fig. 128). On the ceiling is Jupiter between Juno and Minerva, by Paolo Sarti, chiaroscuro decoration is by Castagnoli. Under the baldaquin is the *Throne* that served for the swearing in of the kings of Italy. On the walls are *Gobelins* from the series of *Esther*, portraits by Sustermans and François Paurbus the Younger. The forniture is in Empire style and the vases are Oriental.

Room 7. Blue Room. So called because of the color of the upholstery fabric. On the walls are the Gobelins tapestries showing the *Triumph of the Gods*, from cartoons by Noel Cypel. The portraits are by Sustermans and represent members of the Medici family. A Chinese vase is on the fireplace.

Room 8. Chapel. It was decorated in the XVII cent., with partial modifications done in the neo-classic era. The *Medici portraits* are by Sustermans. Near the window is a *Madonna and Child*, by Dolci, with the frame made of cornelian. Next to it is a beautiful cabinet done in ebony, ivory and alabaster.

Figs. 125-126 - Room of Venus - Rubens: Landscape - Titian: the Concert

Room 9. Of the Parrots. So called because of the parrots that decorate the brocade of the walls. The two tapestries belong to the famous series of the *Triumph of the Gods*. This room was the ante-chamber of Queen Margherita's Appartment, which was separate from that of King Umberto I. On the left wall: *Portrait of Giulia Varano, Duchess of Urbino* by Titian.

On the right wall, Portrait of Francesco I by Hans von Aachen. The stove is Austrian. Next are the Appartments of Queen Margherita.

The appartments of Queen Margherita

Room 10. Yellow room. It is decorated with yellow brocade and splendid Gobelins tapestries (1735-45) showing *hunting scenes of the court of Louis XV*, from cartoons by J.B. Oudry. The Florentine mosaic table with daisies in chalcedony intarsia was donated to the Queen by her Ladies-inwaiting.

Room 11. Bed chamber. On the walls are four other tapestries from the series of the *Hunt of Louis XV*. Portraits are by Sustermans and by Paurbus. The furniture is in Empire style, the *Table and Kneeler* are of Florentine mosaic. Other rooms follow but unfortunately are closed to the public. Perhaps the sumptuous Queen's drawing-room will be visible with its splendid brocades inspired by Chinese art. We return to the Room of the Parrots to continue on the right in the

Appartments of King Umberto I

Room 12. King's Bed chamber. Among other works on the walls: Tapestry from the series of the *Triumph of the Gods*, and *Medici portraits* by Sustermans. The kneeler is of semi-precious stones, the large Austrian stove decorated in stucco.

Room 13. Study. Enriched with brocades, mirrors, lamps and a *Portrait of Claudia dei Medici* by Sustermans.

Romm 14. Drawing room. A particularly interesting work is the Tapestry of the series of the Hunt of Louis XV.

Room 15. Ante-chamber. On the walls are four small XVI cent. Florentine tapestries by Giovanni Roost, from cartoons by Bronzino. On the table is a marble bust representing a *young portrait of Queen Margherita* by Pagliaccetti (1869). Followed by a small landscape with a view of the Boboli Garden, through the corridor on the left we enter

the Room of Bona 16. It was entirely frescoed by Poccetti, who represented, on the walls: 1) Defeat of the city of Bona in Africa 2) Defeat of Prevesa in Albania 3) Silvio Piccolomini announces the taking of Bona to Cosimo II; 4) View of the Port of Leghorn; in the vault, *Apotheosis of Cosimo I*. Observe the two large and va-

Fig. 127 - White room (Royal Appartments)
Fig. 128 - Throne Room (Royal Appartments)

luable chandeliers from Bohemia.

Room 17. Ball-room, (fig. 127)) called the *White Room* because of the stuccoes that decorate it. The architecture is by Gaspare Maria Paoletti (XVIII cent.), the stupendous stucco decoration by the Albertolli. Brothers of Lugano (1776-80). On the door are two Faunas by Innocenzo Spinazzi. This room with its beautiful *chandeliers from Murano*, that at the time of the Savoy was used for grand balls, is now reserved for concerts and above all for the famous High-fashion shows that are held every year in April and November. For the exit (since it is not yet possible to go out from this side), we continue on in the Gallery passing through rooms 1 2 and 3 containing antique statues and Medicean tapestries with episodes about the family. From the windows we can enjoy splendid views of the Boboli Garden and the Fortress Belvedere, farther ahead.

Room VII. Of the Stove (last room of the Gallery). So called because of the large stove that was found here. The walls, frescoed by Pietro da Cortona (1637-40) represent the *Four Ages of the Earth*: Gold, Silver, Bronze and Iron. On the ceiling the Cardinal Virtues and the Great Knigdoms are by Matteo Rosselli (1622). On the floor, the *Triumph of Bacchus* in ceramic (damaged from wear), work of Benedetto Bocchi (1640).

Room VIII. Of Jupiter, from the ceiling subject, frescoed by Luigi Catani 1819). Here are displayed: a *Caricature on Copper* by Callot, *Judith with the Head of Holofernes* by Allori, and the famous *Sleeping Cupid* (fig. 133) by Caravaggio, rendered with luminous plasticity.

Room IX, Bathroom, in Empire style, work of Cacialli (XIX cent.).

Room X. Of Ulysses (see plan). The name of the room derives from the ceiling fresco by Martellini (XIX cent.), with Stories of Ulysses. The fresco symbolizes the return of the Lorraine to Florence after the Napoleonic invasions. Among the works are: *Mary Magdalen* by Dolci; the *Madonna dell'Impannata* (because of the window motif) by Raphael and helpers; *Ecce Homo* by Cigoli and a *Portrait of Andrea Frisier* by Tintoretto. On the wall (perhaps temporarily) is the gracious *Bacchus* (fig. 131) by Reni, inspired by Caravaggio. Farther ahead in the small corridor is

Room XI. Of Prometheus. So named because of the subject of the ceiling by Collignon (1830). Among the most notable works in the room is the large tondo (fig. 132) by Fra Filippo Lippi, Botticelli's teacher, representing *the Madonna and Child, Meeting of St. Anna and Joachim at the Golden Gate and the Birth of the Virgin*. Below, the delicate Dance of Apollo with the Nine Muses is by Giulio Romano, pupil of Raphael. On the right (see plan) follow:

Corridor XII of the Columns: here are graceful works of the Dutch

Fig. 129 - View of the Amphitheater in the Boboli Gardens

and Flemisch schools including *Orpheus in Hell* by Breughel and, at the end, a *Portrait of Maria Ludovica with her Husband*, the Elector Palatine by Douven. Also observe other interesting works identified by their relative plates.

Room XIII. Of Justice. It takes its name from the allegorical fresco of the ceiling, by Fedi (1830). On the walls, *The Savior* and the *Portrait of Tommaso Mosti*, by Titian (both restored). *Portraits of a Gentleman and Lady*, by Moroni; works by Tintoretto, Bassano Veronese and others. On the easel is a realistic *portrait of Anna Maria Ludovica*, the last Medici, by Douven.

Room XIV. Of Flora. Named for the subject of the ceiling, by Marini (1830). On the walls: famous *Stories of Joseph*, by Andrea del Sarto, *Martyrdom of St. Agatha*, by the Venetian painter Sebastiano del Piombo, and *portraits* by Bronzino. In the center of the room is the *Italic Venus*, by Canova, whose model was Paolina Borghese, Napoleon's sister and wife of Prince Borghese.

Room XV. Of the Putti. So called because of the ceiling subject, also by Marini. In this room are works of Flemish and Dutch artists. Among these are: *Girl with a Candle*, by Schalcken; *the Three Graces*, by Rubens; *Hunting Scenes, Seascapes, Flowers and Fruit* by Rachel Ruysch. From the window is a splendid view of the city with the Palazzo Vecchio and, in the background, the hills of Fiesole.

Figs. 130-131 · The Volterrano Appartments · Zocchi: Young Michelangelo · Reni: Bacchus

Room XVI. Of Poccetti, who, in 1620, decorated the ceiling with the Triumphs of Ferdinand I of the Medici. Among the most important works, on the wall near the door, is the realistic Martyrdom of St. Bartholomew, by Ribera, nicknamed "lo Spagnoletto", whose painting shows clear Caravaggesque derivation. Against the wall is a Florentine mosaic table.

Room XVII. Music Room (see plan). Called also room of the drums because of the tables against the walls, made in the form of drums. On the ceiling is the *Liberation of Vienna from the Turks* (1683), vast chiaroscuro fresco by Luigi Ademollo (1819), with a search for optical effects.

In the center is the large Russian malachite table on a gilded bronze base by Pierre Thomire (1819).

Room XVIII. Costagnoli Hall (see plan). From the name of the artist who decorated the room in chiaroscuro (1754-1832). In the center is a rich mosaic table (1815) representing, on the top, the *Triumph of Apollo* and the nine muses and, on the base, the *Four Seasons* in bronze by Dupré. From the window is a view of Ammannati's Courtyard (fig. 129) and the Amphitheater in Boboli.

Room XIX-XXIII. Appartments of Volterrano, so-called because of the artist Franceschini da Volterra (XVIII century), who decorated

Fig. 132 - Room of Prometheus - Filippo Lippi: Madonna and Child

147

the ceiling of the first room with Allegories. On the walls are works by the same artist and Giovanni da San Giovanni. In the center of the room is a statue of *Michelangelo as a Young Boy Sculpting the Mask of a Faun* (fig. 130) by Zocchi (XIX cent.).

Room II. Of Vorterrano. Among the XVII cent. works we point out the painting of *Mary Magdalen* and *St. Francis in Adoration* against the solidary cliffs of the Verna landscape, by Cigoli.

Room of Hercules. On the walls, the *Labors of Hercules*; on the ceiling, *Hercules Received on Olympus*, frescoes of large proportions painted by Pietro Benvenuti (1829).

Among the XVIII cent. works we point out: the realistic *Wild Boar Hunt*, by Snyders; *Adam and Eve*, by Furini and *Narcissus* by Curradi. In the center of the room is a magnificent Sévres Vase that Napoleon gave to Duke Ferdinand III of Lorraine. The last rooms have small interesting works by Salvator Rosa.

The classical entrance, the monumental staircase which leads to the first floor and its beautiful vestibule with a magnificent carved ceiling, were built during the Savoy reign, by Luigi del Moro (1897). In the center of the vestibule is a gracious fountain by Tribolo, sculptor and architect of the Boboli Garden. On the easal is the famous *St. Sebastian*, a superb idealization of a man placed in the vast and splendid Leonardesque landscape, work of Antonio Bazzi called "il Sodoma" from Vercelli (1525).

If open, pass into the second *Vestibule*, with its enormous porphyry basin, where, on the left, begins Vasari's corridor. Farther ahead we go out onto the *vast terrace* with its splendid view of the Palace and the city.

MUSEUM OF SILVERWARE

Open (subject to changes) Mondays, Wednesdays and Fridays, and the second, fourth and fith Sundays of the month, on alternate days with the Royal Appartments. The first rooms were entirely frescoed by the Bolognese Michele Colonna (1640) with a search for optical effects. Among the numerous, incomparable art treasures we can admire in the glass case of

Room I. Gilded silver *cups*, engraved with biblical and mythological figures, Bavarian art of the XVI and XVII cents.

Against the walls: *cabinet* with figures of Johan Wilhem the Elector Palatine; a *Kneeler* from the Manufactory of Pietre Dure; *Madonna of the Rosary*, engraved on a large silver plate and precious engravings of the German Schongaver. On the center table, group of putti by Bernini (XVI cent.). Near the door is a bronze Crucifix of the school of Giambologna.

Room II. In the first case, mitre and lappets embroidered with peacock feathers, work of Mexican art, gift of Charles V to Clement VII. In the other cases are valuable sacred objects. Observe the interesting frescoes of the walls and ceiling by Colonna.

Room III. Cabinet (stipo) of Alemagna, containing sacred vestments, liturgical instruments, and a tiny organ, used (it is believed) by Cardinal Leopold to celebrate Mass. Against the walls are magnificent Florentine mosaic tables.

Room IV. (fig. 135). The largest room, entirely frescoed by Giovanni da San Giovanni and Furini (1635) to glorify the Medici, above all, *Lorenzo the Magnificent among the Muses* and in his *Villa of Careggi*. Among the art treasures displayed in this room are: in the first case, rare rock crystal cups, some with covers of gold with enamelled arabesques; in the third case, vases of amathyst, sardonyx and jasper (plate XXIV), belonging to Lorenzo the Magnificent; the lapis-lazuli vase was designed by Buontalenti (1583). In the case against the wall are gold works from Salzburg and Bavaria. Among the marble busts is one of *Marie Antoniette.* Against the other wall is a *rectangular table* of lapis lazuli. Near the door is a bronze Crucifix from Giambologna's school.

Fig. 133 - Room of Jupiter - Caravaggio: Sleeping Cupid

Fig. 134 - Boboli Gardens: "Viottolone" (Large Lane)

Room. V. Florentine tapestries with *stories of Clement VII*. In the two cases on the left are rare works in crystal decorated with historical scenes. On the right are steps that were destined for the altar that the Medici had projected for the "Chapel of the Princes" in S. Lorenzo, where, in more modern times, an altar was erected which differed from the one originally planned.

Room VI. Treasure Room. (Unfortunately this room is presently closed to the public). As can be read on the respective cards, in the first cases on the right and left are rare and *personal jewels* of Anna Maria Ludovica (the last of the Medici). These jewels had been abitrarily taken by the Dukes of Lorraine but were given back by Austria with the Treaty of S. Germain (1926). Near the windows are precious jasper engravings, one representing Apollo. Among the others is a *Portrait of Savonarola* in cornelian. In the small case below, a rock crystal chest, engraved by Valerio Belli with *Stories of the Passion* (1533), that Clement VII gave to his niece Catherine dei Medici on the occasion of her wedding with Henry II. Returning to Room III, from the "stipo of Alemagna", on the right are other Rooms containing: works in amber, mosaic, ivory and precious tapestries etc. A staircase leads to the Mezzanine where, on the right in a number of rooms, precious ceramic and porcelain items of

150

Italian and foreign make, are displayed. On the left side are other cabinets with valuable Chinese and Japanese porcelain.

In the last room can be seen a *portrait of Napoleon I* in Sevrès porcelain, painted by Gerard.

BOBOLI GARDEN (free entrance)

The garden rose on the hillside of Boboli at the request of Eleonora, wife of Cosimo I. It is a vast and splendid Italian style park-garden, that reflects, in every way, the taste of the high Renaissance period (masses of trees treated as architecture, lawns, grottos, fountains etc.).

Begun by Tribolo (1550), it was continued by Ammannati, Buontalenti and Alfonso Parigi. Entering through the *Bacchus Gateway*, at the end of the short walk is the splendid *Grotto of Buontalenti* (1583). In the third grotto is the beautiful Venus by Giambologna. "The prisoners" on the sides of the first grotto are copies of Michelangelo's originals in the "Accademy". Continuing on the right of the garden, the avenue which curves up to the right leads to the large Amphitheater built by the Medici in the XVII century. In the center, the large granite *basin* comes from the Baths of Caracalla. Even the Egyptian Obelisk, reduced in proportion, comes from Rome. From here we can admire the courtyard of the Pitti Palace closed by *the Fountain* called "*of the Artichoke*" work of Tadda and Susini (XVII cent.). On the side of the Palace is the gracious XIX century 'little Palace' called "*La Meridiana*" constructed by Paoletti and Poccianti, ex-private residence of the Savoy. From here is a splendid view of the city and the hills of Fiesole.

Moving up from the Amphitheater we come to the Neptune Pond with the *Bronze Statue* by Lorenzi (1565). Still higher we enter, if open, the *Garden of the Cavaliere*, with the small house and panoramic garden that was the summer residence of Giangastone, the last Medici Grand Duke. Returning to the Neptune Pond, forther ahead to the right we come to the vast space with the magnificent *cedars of Lebanon*. From here begins the "Viottolone" (fig. 134) (large lane), flanked by high cypresses, pines, statues and other small lateral walks, that leads down to the vast and picturesque "Isolotto" (fig. 136) (small island), with the *statue of Ocean* (from an original by Giambologna in the Bargello), and three statues on the base symbolizing the great rivers: *Nile, Euphrates* and *Ganges*.

Fig. 135 - Palatine Gallery - Museum of Silverware - Room IV

Fig. 136 - Boboli Gardens - L'Isolotto, Ocean Fountain (detail)

GALLERY OF MODERN ART

(closed Tuesdays, save changes)

The entrance is through the central door of the Pitti Palace. Ask the doorman information about the opening time of the Gallery and the use of the elevator. The Gallery is located in the numerous vast rooms of the second floor (one time home of the Lorraine), and offers a splendid panoramic view of the city. This important Gallery, founded by the Provisional Government in 1860, was enriched with works belonging to the city galleries, with the group of " Macchiaioli " paintings from the Diego Martelli collection, and with gifts from collectors of modern art. The large collection allows us to admire a rather complete panorama of Italian painting and sculpture from the XIX century to modern times.

Among the artists represented are: Pietro Benvenuti, Canova, Bartolini, Dupré, Ciseri, Bezzuoli, Ussi, Induno, Palizzi, Michetti, Morselli, Mancini, Achille D'Orsi, Trentacoste, Fattori (fig. 138 bis), Lega Abate, Signorini, Cabianca, Boldini, Medardo, Rosso, Sironi, Spadini, Carena, De Chirico (fig. 138) and many others. Among the non-Italians are: Lumbrach, Scheffer Sargent, Durant.

The Gallery is continuously enriched by generous gifts and new acquisitions.

Fig. 137 - Baldassare Franceschini: A joke of the Parson Arlotto

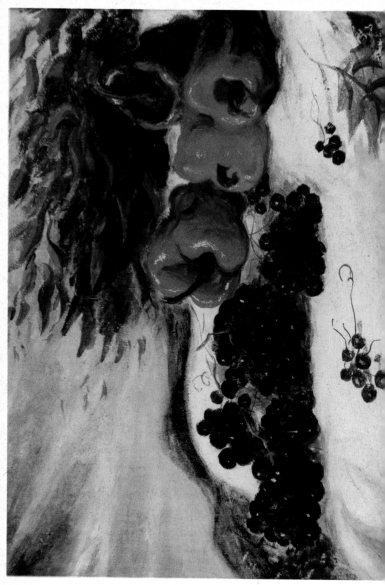

Fig. 138 - Giorgio De Chirico: Still Life

Fig. 138 bis - Fattori: Cart pulled by Oxen ▶

PIAZZA SANTO SPIRITO

(near the Pitti Palace, see plan of the monument N. 15)

On the corner of Via Mazzetta, observe the beautiful *Guadagni Palace* with its splendid *loggia* (1503), attributed to Baccio d'Agnolo or Simone del Pollaiolo called "il Cronaca". This is an example of a typical Renaissance home. The small monument to the agronomist *Cosimo Ridolfi* in the Square is by Raffaello Romanelli (XIX cent.).

Church of S. Spirito (fig. 139). This was Brunelleschi's last creation, begun in 1444, with its typical simple, geometric façade. The *bell-tower* is by Baccio d'Agnolo (1503-17); the *dome* by Salvi di Andrea (1479-81) following a design by Brunelleschi.

Interior. The church is in the form of a Latin cross with three naves that continue in the transept with admirable proportions. Although Brunelleschi's original design underwent some alterations, the church reflects his architectural concept based on harmony of proportions and on the measured division of space.

Along the walls of the church are 38 semi-circular chapels containing the works of art that are listed in the enclosed plan. The beatiful

Fig. 139 - Church of Santo Spirito

PLAN OF S. SPIRITO

A. High altar by Caccini (1608).

B. Vestibule of the Sacristy

C. Sacristy.

D. Offices of the Church

E. Bell-tower by Baccio d'Agnolo

LATERAL CHAPELS

1. Assumption and Saints by Pier Francesco di Jacopo (XVI cent.).
2. "Pietà" copy of 1549 of Michelangelo's in St. Peter (Rome).
3. St. Nicholas of Tolentino, polychrome wood statue attributed to Nanni Unghero.
4. Christ driving the merchants from the temple by Stradano (1572).
5. Incoronation of the Virgin (XVII cent.).
6. Martyrdom of St. Stephen by Passignano.
7. Archangel Raphael and Tobit: marble group by Baratta (XVII cent.).
8. Crucifix with the Virgin and St. John (XVII cent.).
9. Transfiguration by Pier Francesco di Jacopo (XVI cent.).
10. Madonna del Soccorso in the manner of Cosimo Rosselli.
11. Buontalenti Chapel (1601) with small XIV cent. Crucifix.

12. Madonna and Child with Saints and the donors Tanai dei Nerli and his wife with a view of the Ports S. Frediano, by Filippino Lippi (XV cent.).
13. Apparition of the Virgin to St. Bernard, by
14. Marriage of the Madonna (1713). Behind the grating marble sarcophagus of Neri di Gino Capponi (political figure) (1388-1457), by Bernardo Rossellino (1458).
15. Madonna enthroned and Saints in the manner of Lorenzo di Credi.
16. Madonna and child with Saints, XV cent. polyptych.
17. Epiphany by Leoni (XVI cent.).
18. On the altar, Hol Martyrs by Alessandro Allori (1575); in the predella a view of the Pitti Palace before it was enlarged.
19. The Adultress by A. Allori
20. The Blessed Chiara da Montefalco, XVI cent.
21. Annunciation of the XV cent.
22. Nativity (school of Domenico Ghirlandaio).
23. Madonna and Child with Angelo and Saints, XV cent. table with an original frame.
24. St. Monica creating the order of the Augustinian nuns (XV cent.) with an original frame.
25. Madonna and Child with Saints by Cosimo Rosselli (1481).
26. Chapel by A. Sansovino.
27. The Trinity worshipped by St. Catherine and Mary Magdalen, XV cent. attributed to Granacci.
28. Madonna enthroned with Saints, XV cent.
29. Madonna and Child and Saints by Carli (1504).
30. Christ bearing the Cross by Michele del Ghirlandaio. Above, a XV cent. stained glass window representing Incredulity of St. Thomas.
31. Madonna Enthroned with Saints, school of Fra Bartolommeo.
32. Madonna and Saints. Copy of an original by Rosso Fiorentino. XV cent. stained glass window.
33. Entrance to the beautiful vestibule of the Sacristy.
34. Madonna with St. Ann and other Saints by Ridolfo Ghirlandaio
35. St. Thomas of Villanova distributing alms. XVII cent.
36. Blessed Giovanni da S. Fecondo by Masini (1691).
37. Statue of Christ, copy by Landini (1579) of the original by Michelangelo in the Church of Minerva in Rome.
38. Resurrection (XVI cent.).

stained glass window of the inside façade is of the XV century.
In the lateral chapels, entering: *Deposition* and *Christ Resurrected*, copies of originals by Michelangelo in Rome. The Baroque *Tabernacle* of the *Chancel*, by Caccini (1599-1608), is not in keeping with the harmony of the church. Among the paintings observe, in the right trancept, the *Virgin*, commissioned by Tanai de' Nerli, a powerful Florentine and adversary of Savonarola, work of Filippo Lippi; in the apse, *Madonna and Saints* by Lorenzo di Credi; in the last chapel of the choir, on the left: *Nativity*, from the school of Girlandaio. In the left transept, in the first chapel (XXIV): *St. Monica who founds the Order of the Augustinians* by Botticini; in the following chapel, *Madonna and Saints* by Cosimo Roselli. On the following altars are works by XVI century Florentine artists. For architecture and sculpture, observe chapel XXVII, early masterpiece by Andrea Sansovino (1492) who executed, in marble, *the Last Supper*, the Tabernacle and the *Stories of the Virgin.* The balustrade around the Chapel is from 1642. Farther ahead, under the organ, is the entrance to the famous *vestibule*

Vestibule. Projected by Cronaca (Simone del Pollaiolo), it has beautiful corinthian columns that sustain the splendid vault with stone locunars representing the *symbols of the Holy Spirit*. From here we pass to the

Sacristy. Its octagonal shape was inspired by the Baptistry and was built following a design by Giuliano da San Gallo (1489-92). The *Cupola* was constructed from designs by Antonio del Pollaiolo and Salvi d'Andrea. Returning to the Square, on the left of the Church is the entrance to the *Refectory* with a fresco representing the *Last Supper* by Orcagna. This room is also enriched with valuable works of art donated by the antique dealer Salvatore Romano (1946).
In the mornings, the Square with its market and vendors of old things, make this popular quarter particularly interesting.
Farther ahead the short Via St. Monaca, that crosses Via Serragli, leads to the Piazza del Carmine, from where we can admire in the distance, the slim cupola of the Church of S. Frediano, attached to the Seminary of Cestello, by Antonio M. Ferri, following a design by Cerrutti, (1698).

CHURCH OF S. MARIA DEL CARMINE
(see plan of the monuments N. 16)

It was an old Romanesque church from 1268, but was remodelled in the successive centuries, after having been almost totally destroyed by the fire of 1771. Fortunately two chapels were saved; the

Corsini Chapel on the left and, except for the ceiling, the famous Brancacci Chapel in the right transept.

Interior. In the form of a Latin cross with a single nave, it was reconstructed by Giuseppe Ruggeri and Giulio Mannaioni. The ample vault was frescoed, with a search for illusionistic effects in the architecture, by Domenico Stagi. The stained glass window of the inside façade is modern. At the front of the Church, on the right is the *Brancacci Chapel.*

The Brancacci Chapel: it constitutes one of the most solemn monuments of Italian Renaissance painting, because of the cycle of frescoes begun by Masolino da Panicale, continued by Masaccio and finished by Filippino Lippi (see plan) By Masolino da Panicale, Masaccio's teacher, delicate painter of late Gothic style who, in these frescoes, was certainly influenced by his young pupil Masaccio, we can admire: *The Temptation of Adam and Eve*, a great part of *t. Peter healing the cripple* and the *Resuscitation of Tabitha.*

Masaccio continued alone after Masolino left for Hungary and, in opposition to the *Temptation*, represents the *Expulsion of Adam and Eve* (fig. 140) with a new language. Among the most dramatic scenes

Figs. 140-141 - Masaccio: **Adam and Eve** - **Head of christ** (detail of the Tribute)

161

BRANCACCI CHAPEL

1. Expulsion of Adam and Eve from Paradise (Masaccio).
2. Payment of the tribute (Masaccio) (plate LXIX).
3. St. Peter preaching (Masolino).
4. St. Peter baptizing (Masaccio).
5. St. Peter heailng the cripple (Masaccio).
6. St. Peter resuscitates Tabitha (Masolino and Masaccio).
7. Temptation of Adam and Eve (Masolino).
8. St. Paul visits St. Peter in prison (Filippino Lippi).
9. St. Peter resuscitates the Emperor's son (Filippino Lippi).
10. St. Peter enthroned (Masaccio).
11. St. Peter healing with his shadow (Masaccio).
12. St. Peter and St. John giving alms (Masaccio).
13. Crucifixion of St. Peter (Filippino Lippi).
14. St. Peter and St. Paul before the Proconsul (Filippino Lippi).
15. Angel liberating St. Peter from prison (Filippino Lippi).

CAPPELLA BRANCACC

CHIESA DEL CARMINE

g. 142 - Brancacci Chapel - Masaccio: Payment of the Tribute of the Life of St. Peter is the celebrated *Payment of the Tribute* (fig. 142) in which the young Masaccio surpasses his teacher in the powerful, monumental, and vibrantly chiaroscuro figures, full of profound humanty. We can admire the majestic scene in the ample landscape cleared by the light of a recent storm: "Christ the Man dominates the "Apostles" (placed in a semicircle), shown in various attitudes. The story evolves in three times which correspond with three successive scenes. The most important is the one in the center where the Master (fig. 141) orders St. Peter to pay the tribute by taking the money from the mouth of a fish. On the left, the landscape seems to disappear while, on the right the *Scene of the Tribute* is interrupted by the architecture of the buildings. In the scene of *St. Peter Enthroned*, by Masaccio, the young man below that looks out is believed to be self-portrait of the artist. The cycle of frescoes interrupted by Masaccio who went to Rome where he died (1429) was later continued in 1484 by the young Filippino Lippi, who finished the episode of *St. Peter who Resuscitates the Emperor's Grandson* (on the lower left wall; see plan N. 9). By the same artist are: *St. Peter visits St. Paul* in prison (No. 8). On the right wall *Liberation of St. Peter from prison* (15); the young man on the left of the Angel is a self portrait of Filippino Lippi, who also executed *St. Peter and St. Paul before the Proconsul* and the *Crucifixion of St. Peter*, in which in the group of the *three young men*, he painted *a rare portrait of Botticelli (in profile)*, his teacher, while the hillside of Bellosguardo is represented in the background. The scenes finished by the young Filippino, although quite different from Masaccio's drama and Masolino's archaism, are nonetheless enlivened by the artist's sensitivity, expecially acute in the physiognomical and psycological details of the personages. On the altar is an interesting *Madonna and Child* of the XIV cent.

Leaving the Chapel, the vestibule on the right leads to the vast XV cent. Sacristy, containing works by Andrea da Firenze. The frescoes on the walls are by Bicci di Lorenzo representing *scenes* from the life of St. Cecilia.

Returning to the church, in the choir is the monument of Soderini Gonfalonier of the Republic (he is buried in Rome), work of Benedetto da Maiano. In the left wing is the Chapel of S. Andrea, bishop of Fiesole (1302-73), built by Silvani (1683). The Church has a beautiful XVII century cloister, now being restored.

FOURTH ITINERARY

Piazza S. Firenze – Bargello Palace, National Museum – Church of Badia Fiorentina – Dante's House – Square and Church of S. Croce, Pazzi Chapel – Casa Buonarroti. (This itinerary is indicated by numbers 17, 18, 21 and 22 on the map of the monuments.)

SQUARE AND CHURCH OF SAN FIRENZE

On the right, the large Baroque building, originally a convent of the Order of Filippo Neri, was built by Pier Francesco Silvani and Pietro da Cortona (XVII-XVIII cents.). Great part of the building is now the seat of the Tribunal. In the interior is the beautiful Courtyard by Borromini.

On the corner of Via Gondi is the Gondi Palace, with the magnificent courtyard by Giuliano da Sangallo (1490-94), a splendid example of a wealthy residence. Leonardo da Vinci lived here as a guest of the family.

PALACE OF THE BARGELLO (fig. 143)

A Fortress-Palace it was begun in 1255 as the seat of the Captain of the People. The architect of his building, still unknown, incorporated into the palace the existent embattled tower of the "Volognana" with its historic bell that announced the capital punishments with its dismal toll, and that now rings on the occasions of national or local holidays.

From 1261 the palace was the seat of the Podestà, the magistrate whose role was to maintain equilibrium between the parties, and later of the Giudici di Rota. From 1574 it was the seat of the Bargello or Captain of Justice. In this period the interior of the Palace was transformed into squallid and harsh prisons, located on the ground floor, in the "Loggia" and in the "Salone" (Great Hall), then divided in 4 floors with more than 30 cells. At the time of the Podestà, the Hall was the seat of the General Council. It is now dedicated to Donatello and contains masterpieces of XV century Florentine sculpture.

In the courtyard the scaffold was located (now replaced by the well). The room which now contains arms as once used for torture. The prisoners were forced to confes using cruel and horrible instruments of torture. Grand Duke Peter of Lorraine abolished these infamous abuses of Justice, the sad prison cells, the scaffold, the instruments of torture that historians remember with horrifying description. With knowledgeable restorarions by Francesco Mazzei (1865-71) the Palace, a splendid example of Florentine Gothic architecture, was brought back to its antique splendor.

Fig. 143 - Palace of the Bargello

NATIONAL MUSEUM

The Museum was started by the Provisional Government of Tuscany who in 1859 began the collection of statues and other works of art originally in the Uffizi, or coming from religious and public buildings which passed over to the State. The art collections were continuously enriched with the generous contributions of Carrand (1888), Ressman (1899), Franchetti (1909) and others, which were added on to the new acquisitions made by the State. Because of the valuable art collections, this Museum is considered among the most important, especially for Renaissance sculpture.

Room of Arms. Dedicated to the rich collection of arms. This room is severe with wide vaults supported by robust pilasters. On the wall is a restored XIV century fresco of the *Madonna and Saints*. Among the numerous arms: the *Cannon of St. Paul* with the head of the Apostle in its breech, by Cenni (1638). Because of the serious damage caused by the flood, and since the Museum is in the process of reordination and transformation, some works of Michelangelo are temporarily exhibited here and in the small room on the left of the tower. Among these we point out: the *Drunken Bacchus with the*

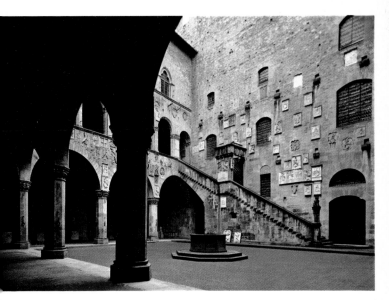

Fig. 144 - Courtyard of the Bargello (National Museum)

small satyr who is *nibbling at the grapes* (1494), the *small David* (not to be confused with the one in the Accademy), the dramatic *Bust of Brutus* and the *Bust of Michelangelo* in bronze by his friend and pupil Daniele da Volterra. In this small room some works from Michelangelo's school are also displayed.

Courtyard (fig. 144). Walking around the courtyard one can better admire the pictorial effect caused by the deep shadows of the harmonious Loggia. The area is rendered solemn by the splendid *staircase*, by Neri di Fioravanti (1345), enriched on high by the beautiful *portal* and *gate* by Giuliano da Sangallo (XV cent.). On the wall are crests of the various Podestà and Giudici di Rota who lived here Under the portico crests of the Quarters and various sections of the city. Of interest is the *lantern* in the form of a cornucopia, in wrought iron by Guido Serafini (XVI cent.). On the other side of the courtyard is the large statue of *Ocean* by Giambologna; *Adam and Eve* by Bandinelli; *Dying Adonis* by Vincenzo Danti; *Virtue suppressing Vice* by Giambologna. In the center of the courtyard is the octogonal well that replaced the scaffold. Opposite to the entrance under the portico we enter the room containing XIV century sculpture. Returning to the courtyard, on the left is a more conmfortable staircase that leads to the **first floor**, in the **Hall of the Ivories** Among the most important works we point out, near the window, a rare French *chess board* from the Carrand Collection and, against the entrance wall, *Madonna and Child* (Umbrian art of the XIV-XV cent.) On the left we enter the

Room of the left of the Balcony. It contains precious liturgical objects of XIV-XV cent. Tuscan art, a *reliquary bust* of St. Ignatius and a *silver cross* (Tuscan art of the XVI cent.).
On the left is the ample

Hall of the Majolicas. In the first case: rare *Spanish-Moorish majolicas* with metallic reflections; in the other cases are ceramics made in Florence, Urbino, Pesaro etc. in prevalence of the XVI cent. At the end of the room: *Credence* in walnut with intarsia design, Florentine art. XVI cent.; above is a *Garland* with the insignias of the Bartolini and Medici families, in *glazed terra cotta* by Giovanni della Robbia. Returning to the previous room, we then pass (as shown in table LXX) to the splendid

Loggia or Balcony that contains works by the Flemish artist Giambologna (1524-1608). Among these is the elegant Mercury (fig. 145), in which we notice the torsion and the thrust of the body, typically manneristic. Farther ahead we enter the

Fig. 145 - Giambologna: Mercury
Fig. 146 - Donatello: Young David in bronze
Fig. 147 - Cellini: Ganymede
Fig. 148 - Donatello: St. George

169

Great Hall with the cross vaults supported by robust octagonal pilasters that, in height, occupies the two floors which was once the seat of the Grand Council at the time of the Podestà. The Hall is now dedicated to the sculptures of Donatello, among which stands out, in the niche of the far wall, *St. George* (c. 1410 - fig. 148) originally in the church of Orsanmichele, perhaps the first Renaissance work of the Master. Also on display by this great artist is the David in bronze (c. 1430 - fig. 146), soft and palpitating, showing his attentive observation of reality. It can be considered an idealized portrait of a Florentine urchin. By Donatello is the youthful *St. John the Baptist* in marble, made for the Martelli family (c. 1440). On the right of the St. George, a realistic bust with a medallion, inspired by classical art, that because of its bold plasticity, is called the "*son of Gattamelata*". On the left is a *Crucifixion* from the artist's last period; next is a *bust of St. John*, by Desiderio da Settignano. On the right wall, famous bronze reliefs representing the *Sacrifice of Isaac* by Brunelleschi and Ghiberti, made for the contest for the second doors of the Baptistry. The confrontation of these two panels is particularly interesting. Between these two panels is a bas-relief representing a *Battle of Roman and Barbarian soldiers* by Bertoldo, teacher of Michelangelo. Below a bronze reliquary chest by Ghiberti. Against the opposite wall are two bas-reliefs in marble and one in colored terra cotta by Agostino di Duccio. Around the sides of the room are delicate works by Desiderio da Settignano and other artists. By Donatello we also mention the *David* and young *St. John* in marble, the *Lion* (Marzocco) in stone believed to be a copy of a lost original. Last finally, by Donatello, is the smiling bronze *Putto*. On the entrance wall is a Madonna and Child by Michelozzo. By Luca della Robbia (1400-82) we admire the *Madonna della Mela* (fig. 149), the *Madonna del Roseto* and two marble bas-reliefs, with episodes from the *Life of St. Peter*. By the Sienese painter and sculptor Vecchietta (1412-80) is the bronze sepulchral statue of Mariano Sozzino, a Sienese judge. From the far end of the room we pass to the

Tower Room (Sala della Torre). In the cases: a rich collection of Roman and Medieval seals, civil and ecclesiastical seals of modern times and *papal and Venetian lead seals*. On the walls are rugs, tapestries and rich fabrics from the Carrand collection.
Following on the right is the

Hall of the Podestà. In this room the Podestà rendered justice. Also called room of the Duke of Athens because, during the restorations, his crest with the "two-tailed Lion" came to light, having been covered after his expulsion (1343). In the center of the room is a

Fig. 149 - Luca della Robbia: Madonna
Fig. 150 - Giotto: Portrait of Dante Alighieri

bronze bust of the collector Carrand (1888) who willed to the Museum furniture, *German, Flemish and Italian paintings*, rare and precious objects from XV and XVI century *Arab art*. Also displayed are exquisite statuettes and wrought gold objects from Italian, French and Flemish art of the XIV-XVII centuries. In the glass cases at the end are XVI cent. Limoges enamels, and XV-XVII cent. glass crystal. Next is the

Chapel of the Podestà. It has a barrel vaulted ceiling, illuminated by acute arched windows, and is where the condemned passed their last night in prayer. The frescoes represent: on the opposite wall, *Vision of Paradise*; on the lateral walls, Scenes from the life of the Madonna and *St. John the Baptist*; on the entrance wall, *Vision of Inferno*. These frescoes which were whitewashed during the plague of 1630 and brought to light by the English scholar Seymone Kirkup in 1839-40, wewre badly restored by Martini and have lost all their iconographical value. Even in the Vision of Paradise, attributed to Giotto, the *portrait of Dante* (fig. 150) has been altered. Below, in the corner, is a *bust of the Poet* (Dante), designed by Kirkup. Here also is Dante's death mask in colored terra cotta. Below the Paradise fresco on the left, *St. Jerome*, fresco by Bartolommeo di Giovanni. On the right, *Madonna and Child,* by Mainardi (1490), and in the

Figs. 151-152 - Cellini: Bust of Cosimo I - Andrea della Robbia: Little Boy

center, table representing the *Madonna and Child between St. Francis and St. John the Baptist*, by Giovanni Francesco (V cent.), from the Carrand collection.

The magnificent lateral choir-stalls and central lectern, originally in San Miniato, are by Bernardo della Cecca (1438-98). In the cases against the entrance wall, Missals in two volumes, by Gherardo and Monte di Giovanni (XV cent.); above, four inlaid wood candelabras, end of XV century; right, *Pietà*, attributed to Jacopo della Quercia. Returning to the Hall of the Ivories, farther ahead on the left is the staircase leading to the

Second floor in te Room of Cellini and Giovanni della Robbia.

By Cellini, goldsmith and sculptur, who also wrote a famous "Autobiography" we admire, on the left: small portrait of Grand Duke Francesco I, donated to his second wife Bianca Capello, with the card that accompanied the gift; the *Liberation of Andromeda*, bronze bas-relief that originally decorated the base of the Perseus in the Loggia della Signoria, which has been replaced with a copy. Next is an oval plaque with a bas-relief o a *greyhound*. Against the following wall, *wax and bronze models* of the *Perseus*. Between these is a large *bronze bust of Cosimo I* (fig. 151), formerly in the fortress of Portoferraio. On the right, *Apollo*, *Hyacinth* and *Narcissus*, marble statues from the Boboli Gardens (deteriorated by the wheather).

Fig. 153 - Bargello (third floor) - Verrocchio: Bronze David

On the right wall, two refined *Ganymedes*, one is a restored classical statue, and the other, done in bronze by Cellini, has the typical manneristic elegance. The room also contains works by Giovanni della Robbia (1469-1529), son of Andrea and nephew of Luca. With his popular type work, Giovanni puts an end to the highest level reached by glazed terra-cotta. (Because of reordinations in course some works by Cellini and Michelangelo that we have mentioned could be temporarily found in other rooms.) Ahead, to the right is the

Hall of bronzes and seals. Dedicated to the artists particularly noted for their small bronzes. We mention those of Riccio, Bellano, Antico, Bandinelli, Giambologna, Francavilla, Soldini, Pietro di Barga and others. The cases contain precious collections of small Italian plaques of the XV and XVI centuries and of *Tuscan coins* from the Republic and Grand Ducal eras. Following is the room dedicated to valuable textiles (donated by Baron Franchetti), generally closed. After this is the

Tower Room, containing realistic wax reconstructions of the *Plague* by Zumbo (1656-1701), perhaps temporarily displayed in the Armory.. Walking toward the entrance, we pass into the

Room of Andrea della Robbia (1435-1525), (nephew of Luca and father of Giovanni), whose splendid terra-cottas are displayed here among them a bust of a boy (fig. 152).

Room of Verrocchio (1435-1588). Sculptor of delicate pictorial effects that constitute the origins of his pupil Leonardo da Vinci's great painting. By Verrocchio is the bronze *adolescent David* (fig 153). Against the left wall *bust of a Gentle Lady with a nose-gay* believed to be Lucrezia Donati, loved by Lorenzo the Magnificent Following are the *death of Francesca Tornabuoni*, *Madonna and Child* and the dramatic *Resurrection* in terra cotta. By Antonio del Pollaiolo (1429-98) is the small *Hercules and Anteus*, with its nervous line suggesting volume and movement. Among the other works in the room are those by Benedetto da Maiano; by Francesco Laurana, *Bust of the Duke of Urbino* rendered with refined geometric abstraction. Against the far wall: among various *portrait-busts of noble Florentines* is the famous rounded with the *Madonna and Child* by Antonio Rossellino. Against the entrance wall, by Mino da Fiesole: marble busts of *Piero and Giovanni dei Medici*; above, Madonna and Child, fine low-relief with traces of gilding. Against the small right wall: *Faith*, *Ecce Homo* and *Portrait of an Unknown gentleman* by the refined Lucchese sculptor Matteo Civitali (1435-1501). At the back, to the left:

Room of the Medal Collections (generally closed to the public). It ontains the precious collection of medals, from the XV to the XIX enturies. Among the most important medals we mention those by Pisanello, Matteo Pasti, Cellini and other artists. Returning to the oom of Andrea della Robbia we enter the Room of the Chimney.

Room of the Chimney. So called because of the splendid XVI century chimney of grey stone that can be seen at the end wall, originally in he Casa Borgherini, enriched with stories of Ciro and Cresa, famous work by Benedetto da Rovezzano. Among other works in this room: *bust of Costanza Bonarelli*, by the great sculptor Gian Lorenzo Bernini (1525-1608); bust of the Dominican friar *Paolo Costabili* by Alessandro Vittoria; near the entrance, *Bacchus and a Faun* by Jacopo Sansovino (restored after it was damaged in a fire). Finally an anatomical figure in bronze by Ludovico Cigoli (1559-1613).
Leaving the Museum, on Via Proconsolo, across the street is:

CHURCH OF THE BADIA FIORENTINA

It was originally a Benedictine church founded in the XI century by Willa, mother of Ugo, Marquis of Tuscany. Enlarge dat the end of the XIII century it acquired numerous additions in the XIV cent. In 1625 it was entirely remodelled by Matteo Segaloni. The entrance

Fig. 154 - House of Dante Alighieri

Fig. 155 - Church of Santa Croce - Giotto: Death of St. Francis

is through the beautiful portal by Benedetto da Rovezzano (1475), surmonted by a *Madonna and Child* in glazed terra cotta by Buglioni (early XVI cent.). The Vestibule, consisting of the beautiful portico with Corinthian columns, is by Benedetto da Rovezzano (1495).

Interior of the Church. It is only church in Florence made in the form of a Greek cross. The beautiful carved ceiling is by Gamberai, following the design by Segaloni (1625). On the left wall, *Madonna appearing to St. Bernard*, masterpiece by Filippino Lippi (1485, table). In the left wing *Tomb of Count Ugo, Marquis of Tuscany*, extremely refined work by Mino da Fiesole (1480). Above, *Ascension* by Vasari. On the right wall, *Madonna and Child with St. Lawrence and St. Leonard, delicate altar-back by Mino da Fiesole. In the right* wing: Tomb of Giannozzo Pandolfini, from the school of Rossellino. Dante, who lived nearby, attended this church.

Passing through the choir on the right, we ascend to the upper portico of the *Cloister degli Aranci* (of the Oranges), which was frescoed with *Stories of St. Benedict* by Giovanni Consalvo (XV cent.) (taken away for restoration). A visit to this picturesque cloister is particularly recommended because of the characteristic medieval atmosphere that is conserved here. From here we can best admire the hexagonal *bell-Tower*, attributed to Arnolfo di Cambio, with its XIV cent. Romanesque mullioned windows that terminates with a sharp cusp sustained by the beautiful cornice. Returning to Rovezzano's portico, ahead we exit to Via Dante Alighieri. On the left we reach the nearby little square of St. Margherita where we see the so called *House of Dante*

HOUSE OF DANTE

The house is an arbitrary reconstruction of the last century (fig. 154), and is now used for displaying and selling of contemporary art. On the side of Via St. Margherita, in a medieval environment, we can visit the new Dantesque Museum consisting of documents and curios concerning Dante in Florence and in exile. According to recent documentations, it seems that Dante was born in a house on this little Square of San Martino located on the same side as the restaurant "Il Pennello", so-called because it was opened as a wine cellar by the painter Albertinelli, and was a gathering place for artists of the time. Above the restaurant is the *terra-cotta medallion* with the portrait of the painter who left art to dedicate himself to this business. In the square of S. Martino we see the "Torre della Castagna" (Tower of the Chestnut), that was the seat of the citizens' government, now occupied by offices of the local Magistrate. Opposite is the Church of SAN MARTINO where Dante married Gemma

Donati. The tiny church was reconstructed in the XV century. On the inside walls are frescoes with *stories of S. Martino and works of Charity*, by Domenico Ghirlandaio and Filippino Lippi. Here St. Antonino, beloved bishop of the Florentines, founded the famous "Compagnia dei Buonomini" who effectively helped the poor families and those of fallen fortune in the most unobtrusive manner, without humiliating the beneficiaries as stated in the Gospel: "that the right hand should not know what the left hand does".

Walking along the Via dei Magazzini, with its medieval buildings, we arrive at the nearby Via Condotta, with its old "tower-houses". Turning to the left we reach Piazza S. Firenze. Crossing the street, alongside the church, is the Via dell'Anguillara that crosses, ahead on the right, the picturesque Via Filippina. Still farther ahead is Via Bentaccordi, where on the façade of the modest house on the right corner, a plaque commemorates the place where Michelangelo lived as a boy. On the left, the beautiful palace that curves on the small Via Torta, rises on the external line of the Roman theater which once stood here. Ahead is the

PIAZZA SANTA CROCE

On the left corner at the beginning of Via Verde, observe the beautiful Serristori Palace, formerly Cocchi, by Baccio d'Agnolo (c. 1520, now a school). Across the street, at the beginning of the square, is a gracious fountain (XVI cent.), used as a watering place for horses.

On the right is the large Palazzo dell'Antella, formerly Cerchi Palace (1619), with its façade frescoed by Giovanni da San Giovanni and helpers (according to legend, in only 20 days).

Observe this palace and the one beside it that rest on corbels and are thrust onto the square. Under the corbels of the first palace is a bust of Cosimo II (perhaps in restoration because of damage caused by the flood); below is a marble disk dated February 10, 1565 that marks the central point of the field when the soccer game was played in the square. In medieval times great crowds gathered in this famous square to hear the sermons of followers of St. Francis, among whom was St. Bernardine of Siena. Among the famous jousting taurnaments held here, we mention that in honor of the "handsome Giuliano" Medici, presided over as queen by the "beautiful Simonetta", immortalized by Botticelli in his "Springtime" and "Birth of Venus" in the Uffizi.

Fig. 156 - Church of Santa Croce (Holy Cross)

CHURCH OF SANTA CROCE

The church was begun, it is believed, by Arnolfo in 1294, on the site of an older church. The mediocre FAÇADE by Niccolò Matas (1845-63 - fig. 156) contrasts with the simple and austere construction. The statues that decorate it are: by Giovanni Duprè, the *Madonna* above the central portal and the *Triumph of the Cross* in the lunette below; by Zocchi is the *Vision of Costantine* in the lunette of the right door; by Tito Sarrocchi is the *Discovery of the Cross* in the lunette of the left door.

The sandstone Gothic-style bell towewr is by Baccani (1874). On the left side is the beautiful XIV century portico in the same style as the one on the right, visible when entering the cloister. To the left of the façade is the mediocre monument dedicated to Dante Alighieri, by

Fig. 157 · Church of Santa Croce · Interior
Fig. 158 · Donatello · Wooden Crucifix (detail)

Enrico Pazzi (1865), which originally encumbered the center of the square but was removed in May 1968, and placed here after much controversial discussion.

Interior (fig. 157). It is in te form of a "T", its length is 115,43 meters, width 38,23 meters, width of the transept 73 meters. It is a vast and very simple church capable of holding the population of this crowded quarter. A solid construction, its octagonal stone pillars prolonged by strips sustains the beautiful trestled ceiling. The simple chapels in the transept accentuate the vertical value of the wide central nave and the pictorial effect is extended to the lateral naves by means of the succession of transversal arches that sustain the beautiful vault with the sloping roof.

Originally all the walls were frescoed by the most famous XIV century artists. Cosimo I, after becoming absolute ruler of the city and insensitive to the glories of the past, had the famous frescoes covered with whitewash, and had Vasari add the heavy altars (with XVII cent. paintings) that contrast with the harmony of the church. Because of these alterations the frescoes were lost except for a few fragments that are conserved in the Museum in the Cloister. Before the church was declared "Pantheon of the nation's glories", many noble families were buried here thus reaching the number of 280

Fig. 159 - Benedetto da Maiano: Pulpit with stories of St. Francis

PLAN OF THE CHURCH OF SANTA CROCE

Interior of the Church

tombs. Now only great Italians can be buried here; the last of these being inventor Barsanti buried in 1954.

Central nave. On the third pillar (see plan N. 1) is the famous *pulpit* (fig. 159) by Benedetto da Maiano (1472-76) with panels representing the *Stories of St. Francis* (inspired by those of Ghiberti) and the *Cardinal Virtues* below.

Right nave. Tomb of Michelangelo (fig. 160), by Vasari (1570). The figures of *Painting, Sculpture* and *Architecture* are by Lorenzi, Cioli and Giovanni dell'Opera (XVI cent.). The *bust of the Artist* was taken from his death mask. In front of the tomb, on the first pillar, Madonna and Child called "of the milk" (fig. 161), a delicate low-relief by Antonio Rossellino (1578). Between the second and third altars, a *Cenotaph to Dante Alighieri* (who died and is buried in Ravenna), by Stefano Ricci (1829); between the third and fourth altars, monument to Vittorio Alfieri by Canova (1810), in neo-classic style; between the fourth and fifth altars, *Tomb of Niccolò*

Fig. 160 · Vasari: Tomb of Michelangelo
Fig. 161 · Antonio Rossellino · Madonna "of the milk"

Machiavelli, by Innocenzo Spinazzi (1787), with the profile of Machiavelli on the plaque being held by the allegorical figure of *Diplomacy*.

After the tomb of the art historian Luigi Lanzi, is the celebrated *Tabernacle by Donatello* (fig. 162) in gilded grey-stone (pietra serena), with the magnificent *Annunciation*, and above, vivacious *putti* in terracotta. Following is the *tomb* of the humanist and chancellor of the Florentine Republic Leonardo Bruni, that became the prototype of Renaissance tombs because of its harmony and serene composition. Next is the tomb, by Cassioli, of Gioacchino Rossini who died in Paris and was transported here in 1866. Finally, by Berti (1936), is the *statue of Ugo Foscolo* who sang the praises of Santa Croce in his poem "Sepulcri", and who is buried under the floor, as indicated by the inscription.

Right wing of the transept. *Tomb of Prince Neri Corsini*, by Fantacchiotti.

Castellani or Sacrament Chapel. This chapel still conserves a great part of the XIV century fresco decoration. On the right wall: *Stories of St. Nicholas of Bari and St. John the Baptist*; on the left are stories of St. John the Evangelist and St. Anthony Abbot, all by Agnolo Gaddi, son of Taddeo, and helpers. The crucifix is by Niccolò di

Fig. 162 - Church of Santa Croce - Donatello: Annunciation

Pietro Gerini (1386). On the left entrance wall, surmounted by a very fine grating with figures of the *Archangel and the Virgin* is the *tomb* of a member of the Giugni family, attributed to the Sienese Balduccio (XIV cent.).

Baroncelli now Giugni Chapel. The famous frescoes, which have been carefully restored, are by Taddeo Gaddi (1332-38), faithful pupil of Giotto, who represented *Stories from the Life of the Virgin* showing a fine ability for narration. On the right end wall, Madonna of the Girdle, by Sebastiano Mainardi (XV cent.). Leaving this chapel to the right we pass the beautiful portal and enter the corridor with the barrel vaulted ceiling and elegant mullioned windows, by Michelozzo who, in 1434, also built the Chapel at the end called "Novitiate" or "Medici" Chapel, because it was built for Cosimo the Elder. The harmonious chapel contains various Della Robbia works. On the right of the corridor is the entrance to the *Sacristy*. On the walls are *Stories of the Passion*, frescoes attributed to Niccolo di Pietro Gerini (end of the XIV cent.). Separated by the "wrought-iron gate" is the small

Rinuccini Chapel. It was frescoed by Giovanni da Milano and helpers (c. 1365), with *Stories of Mary Magdalen* on the right wall; *Stories of Mary* on the left wall; and in the vault, the Savior and the *Evangelists*. Among the collaborators we mention the one known to the critics as the "Master of the Rinuccini Chapel", whose style is near to that of Nardo di Cione. On the alter is a *polyptych* with the *Madonna, Child and Saints* by Giovanni del Biondo (1397).

Returning to the church we mention the fact that the eleven chapels in the trancept were altered or remodelled in the XIV century by the noble families for their burial places.

I. VELLUTI CHAPEL. Conserves fragments of XIII century frescoes with Legends of St. Michael the Archangel.

II. CALDERINI CHAPEL later Riccardi. Vault was frescoed by Giovanni da S. Giovanni.

III. GIUGNI CHAPEL later Bonaparte. On the left, *tomb of Carlotte Bonaparte* by Lorenzo Bartolini; on the right, *Tomb of Giulia Bonaparte Clary* (d. 1845), by Pampaloni.

IV. PERUZZI CHAPEL. Frescoed by Giotto probably around 1320. It underwent an unfortunate restoration by Marini (1863) and was once again restored in 1965. On the walls, fragments of the *Stories of St. John the* Evangelist; on the sides of the windows, *four Saints*.

V. BARDI CHAPEL. It was entirely frescoed by Giotto after 1317 with *Stories of St. Francis*. Unfortunately even these frescoes, discovered in 1840, were unhappily restored by Gaetano Bianchi. With the restoration of 1965 the parts which were not original were

Fig. 163 - Museum of Santa Croce - Cimabue: Crucifix

removed, leaving those which the experts believe to be by Giotto (who can be appreciated in the fullness of his form in the famous *Madonna*, located in the Uffizi Gallery). Among the remains of these frescoes that narrate the *Stories of St. Francis*, we point out the *Death of the Saint* (fig. 155 pag. 176-177, 1318). The altar-piece with Stories of St. Francis is believed to be by a Florentine artist influenced by Byzantine art (c. 1265).

VI. MAIN CHAPEL. This chapel is rendered light by the verticalism of its form illuminated by tall beautiful stained-glass windows, and was frescoed by Agnolo Gaddi. On the altar, polyptych composed of panels from dismembered works by various Florentine artists of the late XIV century. In the center is the *Madonna* by Niccolò di Pietro Gerini; flanked by *Doctors of the Church* by Nardo di Cione; unknown is the artist of the predella. Above is a large Crucifix by a follower of Giotto. The walls, entirely frescoed by Agnolo Gaddi and followers (1380-85) representing the famous *Legend of the Cross* (fig. 164) narrated with richness of personages, minutely detailed and with the poetic language of Florentine-Gothic painting.

On the right wall the scenes show, from top to bottom: Seth receives a branch from the tree of life from St. Michael. Seth plants the branch on the tomb of Adam. The Queen of Sheba adoring the bridge made from the wood of the tree-Solomon has the tree buried; the Jews extract the tree from the pool in which it is found and make it into a cross; Saint Helena finds the three crosses, among which is the "true Cross" which will be identified by means of a miracle.

On the left wall, from top to bottom: St. Helena carries the cross in procession into Jerusalem; Chosroes, King of the Persians, conquers Jerusalem, carries away the Cross and is adored by his subjects. An Angel announces to Heraclius his coming victory. Heraclius defeats Chosroes and has him beheaded; an Angel appears to Heraclius warning him that he must abondon triumphs and honors; Heraclius gets down from his horse and, carrying the Cross in penitent's robes, enters Jerusalem. In the vault are figures of the *Savior*, the *Evangelists* and *Saint Francis*.

VII. TOLOSINI CHAPEL later SPINELLI AND SLOANE. Remodelled at the beginning of the XIX cent. On the altar is a polyptych of the *Madonna and Saints* by Giovanni del Biondo (XIV cent.). The predella with historical scenes is by Neri di Bicci.

VIII. CHAPEL OF ST. ANN. Restored, it is dedicated to the "Italian mother and to the Unknown Soldier". The monument is by Libero Andreotti (1926).

IX. CHAPEL OF ST. ANTHONY OF PADUA. Renovated in 1826.

X. PULCI CHAPEL later Berardi later BARDI. Frescoes of the Martyrdom of St. Lawrence and the Martyrdom of St. Stephen by

Fig. 165 - Monument to Galileo Galilei
Fig. 166 - Tomb of Giacomo Rossini

Bernardo Daddi and helpers (c. 1330, restored). On the altar a large terracotta work by Giovanni della Robbia showing the *Madonna and Child* between Mary Magdalen and St. John the Evangelist.

XI. BARDI DI VERNIO CHAPEL. On the walls are celebrated frescoes by Maso di Banco (c. 1340, restore) representing *Stories of St. Sylvester* and of *Constantine*: among these, the Miracle of the bull resuscitated by the Saint, *the Dreams of Constantine* with the Vision of SS. Peter and Paul. The *Final Judgement* is from the school of Maso, the Deposition in the manner of Taddeo Gaddi. On the altar, a panel by Jacopo di Cione with *St. Giovanni Gualberto and episodes from his life.*

XII. NICCOLINI CHAPEL, at the end of the transept, closed by the gate, by Giovanni Dosio; the vault was frescoed by Volterrano (XVII cent.).

XIII. BARDI CHAPEL (glosed by the gate). It contains Donatello's famous Wooden Crucifix (c. 1425 - fig. 158 - page 181).

XIV. SALVIATI CHAPEL, rebuilt by Gherardo Silvani (XVII cent.). Contains the harmonious tomb of Princess Sophia Zamoyski Gartoyski, by Bartolini (1840). Descending the steps we see the *Monument to Luigi Cherubini*, musician who died and is buried in Paris, by Fantacchiotti (1869). In front of the first pillar is a *statue of Leon Battista Alberti* by Bartolini (1840). From this spot, observe the beautiful rosewindow of the internal façade with the Deposition.

Left Nave. Monument to the engraver Raffaello Morghen by Odoardo Fantacchiotti (1854). The painting in the next altar is the *Pentacost* by Vasari. The three medallions are in memory of *Christopher Columbus, Amerigo Vespucci* and the astronomer *Paolo Toscanelli.* Following is the famous tomb of *Carlo Marsuppini,* humanist and Secretary of the Florentine Republic, by Desiderio da Settignano (1460), who, inspired by the famous tomb of Leonardo Bruni by Rossellino, directly opposite, made the forms more delicate, as shown by the figures of the children which are considered among the most admirable creations of the Renaissance. In the floor, also by Desiderio, *monumental slab of Gregorio Marsuppini,* father of Carlo. On the wall, above left, fragment of a fresco by Agnolo Gaddi. Following: monument to the great hydraulics engineer and statesman Vittorio Fossombroni (d. 1844), by Bartolini (1850). Ahead is a medallion with a *bust of Donatello* (buried in San Lorenzo). Below: monument to *Carlo Botta.* On the fifth altar, *Ascension* by Stradano (1569). Followed by a Pietà by Bronzino. In the floor, large *monumental slab* (with inscription) of *Lorenzo Ghiberti,* who is buried here with his son Vittorio. The next small slab is of Barsanti, remembered also on the wall above. On the wall follow the plaques of Raphael (buried in the pantheon) and of *Leonardo* (buried in Amboise, France). Finally farther ahead, late XIV century frescoes (very restored) and the tomb of *Galileo Galilei* (d. 1642) erected following the design of Giulio Foggini (fig. 165). The statues of *Astronomy* and *Geometry* are by Vincenzo Foggini and Gerolamo Ticciati; the *bust of Galileo* by Foggini.

Internal façade. The beautiful stained glass rose-window previously mentioned, is by the Florentine Giovanni del Ponte (1399-1437). Below, on the right of the central door, the *monument to the historian Gino Capponi* is by Bortone (1884); on the left of the door, by Pio Fedi (1883) is the *monument to G. Battista Niccolini,* buried between the second and third pillars of the right nave. The statue of *Liberty* that breaks the chains, in remembrance of Niccolini who was a strong advocate of Liberty, inspired Berthold who sculpted the famous Statue of Liberty in New York harbor, offered to America by France. Leaving the church, on the left is the entrance to the Cloister of Santa Croce.

CLOISTER OF SANTA CROCE

The vision offered by this first Cloister (fig. 167) is stupendous, especially on clear mornings. From every angle we can admire the harmonious XIV century construction, closed on the far end by the

Fig. 164 - Old Refectory - T. Gaddi: The Tree of the Holy Cross and the Last Supper

portico of the Pazzi Chapel. Beginning the visit, under the portico on the right, *Tomb of Girolamo Segato* who, dying at the age of 45 years (1835), condemned by the Inquisition, destroyed his invention of the petrification of animals and cadavers. In the niche is the small symbolic monument to Florence Nightengale (born in Florence, 1820-1890), by Sargent. During the restoration, some badly damaged frescoes and numerous plaques that overpowered the XIV cent. style were removed. However the harmony of the Cloister would be further improved if the gross statue of the *Almighty* by Bandinelli were also taken away.

Pazzi chapel (the interior is described farther ahead) with its simple geometric façade left incomplete because of the death of Brunelleschi (1446), who began its construction in 1430. After his death it was continued by his collaborators who left the portico incomplete, resting on corinthian columns, which sustain the high attic divided into squares, interrupted in the center by the perfect curve of the arch. Farther ahead, on the right of the cloister, is the entrance to Museum of the Opera di Santa Croce.

MUSEUM OF THE OPERA DI SANTA CROCE

Many works of this museum were damaged in the flood of November

1966 and are now in restoration. Among these we mention the famous Crucifix by Cimabue (fig. 163). Even though the works are still missing we will mention the most important in the order in which they are usually found. On the left wall a fresco by Domenico Veneziano, originally in the Church, with St. Francis and St. John the Baptist. In a reconstruction of its original niche in Orsanmichele: the gilded bronze statue of St. Ludovic of Toulouse, young work of Donatello (c. 1422), already permeated by Renaissance classicism in the monumental yet sweet figure of the Saint. Proceding ahead, on the right and left walls, are fragments of frescoes taken from the Church. On the end wall of this old refectory is the fresco by Taddeo Gaddi (restored) representing the *Tree of the Holy Cross;* below is the *Last Supper and other Stories.*

In the adjoining small room on the left, seat of the "Theological Studies for Laymen" are fragments of XV century windows; on the end wall, *Dying St. Francis distributes bread to his fellow monks,* fresco by Giovanni da San Giovanni. On the left of this room is a collection of paintings of the XVI and XVII centuries. Returning to the Cloister, farther ahead on the right, through the beautiful portal by Michelozzo or Benedetto da Maiano (c. 1450), we enter the

Second Cloister, that modern critics believe to be by Bernardo Rossellino (1409-64). Moving around this Renaissance Cloister we can better admire the extremely elegant portico surmounted by the light Loggia. From here we can see the "Rotunda" with, on the left, the tower of the *National Library*, one of the most important in Italy, with its entrance on Piazza dei Cavalleggeri, along the river, by Cesare Bazzani (1911-35). The National Library, very badly damaged during the flood, contains the richest collections of manuscripts and literary material printed in Italy. Returning to the first Cloister, observe the tall cusps along the side of the Church, that enrich the XIV century portico closed by the Pazzi Chapel (fig. 167).

PAZZI CHAPEL

Last creation by Brunelleschi, left incomplete: *Entrance portico* with the barrel vaulted ceiling decorated with exquisite rosettes. The delicate *Cherubs* in the friezee are by Desiderio da Settignano; the cupola decoration is by Luca Della Robbia; the beautiful carved wood door is by Giuliano da Maiano (1472).

Interior. Elegant central plan creation; grey stone fluted columns inserted in the white walls, sustain the harmonious cupola. On high the *Lantern*, with its graceful small columns, illuminates the barrel vaults. At the sides are crests of the Pazzi family, represented by dolphins. Even the Evangelists in the polychromed medallions are

Fig. 167 - Cloister of Santa Croce - Brunelleschi: Pazzi Chapel

Fig. 168 - Casa Buonarroti - Façade

Fig. 169 - Michelangelo - Self-portrait

believed to be by Brunelleschi. The beautiful window in the apse with St. Andrew is attributed to Baldovinetti.

Returning to Piazza Santa Croce, the narrow Via dei Pepi leads to the nearby Via Ghibellina, where, at No. 70, indicated by Michelangelo's bust over the door, is the Casa Buuonarroti (fig. 168)

CASA BUONARROTI (fig. 168)

This is not the house in which Michelangelo was born (he was born in the barren and solitary village of Caprese in Casentino, in the province of Arezzo), but rather the one bought by the artist for his nephew Leonardo Buonarroti. It was decorated by Michelangelo's grand-nephew in the XVII century and was transformed into a Museum in 1859, when it was generously given to the city by his successors. In 1964, during the centenary celebrations, Casa Buonarroti was destined as the seat of the "Center of Studies of Michelangelo". After some restorations the Museum, dedicated exclusively to the great artist, was reopened to the public in 1965. Because of the flood damage, many of the works cited on the ground floor are still in restoration.

Entrance. *Bronze bust of Michelangelo*, by Daniele da Volterra. In the rooms on the left are some plaster models of the artist's most famous

Figs. 170-171 - Michelangelo: Madonna of the Stairs - Wooden Christ

sculptures. In the rooms on the right: self-portrait of Michelangelo (fig. 169). In the following rooms: a small picture-gallery of the Buonarroti where, among other works, is the celebrated portrait of Vittoria Colonna, perhaps by Pontormo.

First Floor. Beginning on the left: *Madonna and Child* called *Madonna of the Stairs* (fig. 170), young work by Michelangelo which was inspired by Donatello's bas-relief; on the right, marble relief of the *Battle* of the Centaurs and Lapites, also from the master's youth (c. 1492). Also displayed are two wax models for the David and a terra-cotta model for the Madonna and Child in the New Sacristy in San Lorenzo.

In the room on the left are drawings by Michelangelo and a design for the façade of the Church of San Lorenzo. Continuing on the right: Appartments of Michelangelo's nephew Leonardo with XVII cent. frescoes representing: *episodes from the life of Michelangelo*; among the most important works: *wooden Crucifix* (fig. 171) found in the Church of S. Spirito, and important *designs* for fortifications. Finally we point out the *torso of a river god* in terra-cotta, intended for the Medici Chapels, left incomplete.

Second floor. Reserved for the "Center of Studies of Michelangelo".

FIFTH ITINERARY

Piazza of Santissima Annunziata – Portico and Hospital of the In nocents – Church of SS. Annunziata – Etruscan and Egyptian Mu seums. (Plan of the Monuments N. 23-24.)

PIAZZA SS. ANNUNZIATA

This is the first Renaissance square with a portico of rounded arches designed by Brunelleschi. In the center is the bronze *equestrian statu* of Ferdinand I of the Medici, last work by Giambologna, finished by Tacca in 1608. The decoration of the pedestal, with the *queer bee* and an inscription in honor of Ferdinand I, is from 1640. The two graceful *Fountains* in bronze, with fantastic marine monsters considered among the most important of their kind. are by Tacc and helpers (1629). On the corner of the square and Via dei Serv is the Riccardi Mannelli Palace (with the brick façade) by Amman nati (c. 1577).

PORTICO OF THE HOSPITAL OF THE INNOCENTS

It was begun by Brunelleschi in 1420 (fig. 172), continued and finish ed with slight variations by Francesco della Luna in 1445.
In the spaces above the nine arches are the famous terra-cotta me dallions showing *abbandoned babies in swaddling clothes*, imploring help from their mothers with their innocent gestures, by Andrea Dell

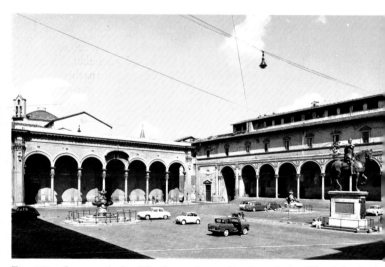

Fig. 172 - Square of the SS. Annunziata - Portico of the Hospital of the Innocents

196

Robbia (1486), beloved nephew and pupil of Luca.

The square, left incomplete because of the death of Brunelleschi, was continued in the central portico by Manetti and Antonio da San Gallo, to whom the central arch is attributed, finished later by Caccini. The portico on the left, by Antonio da San Gallo and Baccio d'Agnolo (1516-25), inspired by Brunelleschi on the opposite side of the square, has the letter "S" in the medallions, referring to the Servite Fathers who officiate the Church.*

Hospital of the Innocents. It was founded in 1421 during the Florentine Republic and is the first institution of its kind in Europe.

Observe, under the portico on the left, the inscription on the closed window surmounted by two putti that recalls the "ruota" (wheel) and was used until 1875. With this device children were left while their mothers remained anonymous. Through the door in the center of the portico is the entrance to the Hospital of the Innocents, with its beautiful courtyard where, in the lunette over the door, is an *Annunciation* in terra-cotta by Andrea della Robbia.

On the right is the entrance to the rooms that contain portraits of the benefactors. Farther ahead is a SMALL MUSEUM, with works by Giovanni del Biondo, Neri di Ricci, Piero di Cosimo and others. Also the famous *Adoration* by Domenico Ghirlandaio (1488), who put his self-portrait in the second figure on the right of the Virgin. From Ghirlandaio's school are: the *Slaughter of the Innocents*, the *Stories of Saints*, the *Passion* and *St. Anthony consecrating the Church of this Hospital*.

CHURCH OF SANTISSIMA ANNUNZIATA

The Church rose on the old Oratory of the Servites of Mary founded in 1235 by seven young nobles who, tired of the fighting between factions, retired here to a life of contemplation. In order to isolate themselves completely from the city, they then found the Monastery of Monte Senario, beyond Fiesole. In the middle of the XV century Michelozzo built the First Cloister. The Church, begun by Michelozzo (1444) and Pagno Partigiani, was modified later by Alberti, at the expense of the Marquis of Gonzaga.

First Cloister. On the walls, the frescoes represent, beginning from right to left: the *Assumption* (1517) by Rosso Fiorentino; the *Visitation* (1516) by Pontormo; *Marriage of the Virgin* (1513) by Franciabigio; *Birth of the Virgin* and the *Adoration of the Magi* by Andrea del Sarto, who portrayed his wife Lucrezia del Fede in the face of the Madonna. After the door, the *Nativity* with its ample landscape by Baldovinetti (1460), badly deteriorated by the weather. Following is *St. Filippo Benizzi assuming the Habit of the Order* by

Cosimo Rosselli. The other *Scenes of the Miracles of the Saint* are by Andrea del Sarto (buried in this church and remembered here with a marble bust). Many of these frescoes have been taken down for restoration.

Interior. It has a single nave with a lage cupola, called the "rotunda", built on a design by Alberti. The deep lateral chapels, fancily decorated in the XVIII century, alter Alberti's construction. The beautiful carved and decorated *ceiling* is by P. Giambelli, following a design by Volterrano (XVII cent.).
Entering on the left is the

Marble Tempietto, designed by Michelozzo (1448-61). It is closed by an exquisite bronze cord grill. The rich votive lamps were donated by the Medici and other faithful. The XVII century *silver altar* portrays a Medici Prince praying. This small temple (tempietto) was erected to honor the miraculous *Annunciation* frescoed on the wall (fig. 173), that, according to legend, was painted by an angel while the XIV century artist was sleeping, worried that he would not be able to represent the Virgin in such a way as to surpass the beauty of the angel that he had already painted. The face of *Christ* on the pyx is by Andrea del Sarto.
In the Chapels on the left of the nave, among the most important works are: *God the Father with St. Jerome* and *The Trinity* by Andrea del Castagno; farther ahead is the *Assumption* by Perugino. In the chapel to the right of the main altar is a *Tomb* with a *Deposition*, by Bandinelli (1559) who is buried here with his wife. At the right of the entrance to the dome, *Tomb* of Donato dell'Antella, who died in 1666, by Foggini. On the left: *Tomb of Bishop Angelo Marzi Medici*, by Francesco da Sangallo (1546). The small monumental stone on the floor indicates where Andrea del Sarto was buried. The *Major Altar*, enclosed by a balustrade, is enriched by a silver ciborium. The fresco of the cupola, representing the *Incoronation of the Virgin*, is by Volterrano (XVII cent.). In the left transept is the

Chapel of Baptism, containing a statue of the *Baptist* in terra-cotta by Michelozzo. From this side we enter the corridor that leads around the tribune, where, among the many surrounding Chapels, is the one at the end called "Cappella del Soccorso" (N. 13 of the plan), that Giambologna created for his tomb and those of his collaborators. It is an interesting chapel with a bronze Crucifix and bronze reliefs with *Scenes of the Passion*, all works of Giambologna.
Leaving the church, on the right, is the entrance to the CLOISTER OF THE DEAD built by Portigiani following a design by Michelozzo (XV cent.). It is called "Cloister of the Dead" because at one

Fig. 173 - **Miraculous Image of the SS. Annunziata** (Unknown Tuscan Artist - XIV cent.)

me great Florentine families were buried here, as shown by the
umerous monumental slabs. In the lunettes: *Stories of the Servites*

Fig. 174 - Etruscan Museum - The Chimera, bronze

of Mary by Poccetti, Matteo Rosselli and other XVII cent. artists
In the lunette above the door of the church (under glass), is the
famous *Madonna del Sacco,* by Andrea del Sarto (1525). In the
corner on the left is the door leading to the *Chapel of St. Luke*
(generally closed). Under the chapel are buried Cellini, Pontormo
Franciabigio, Bartolini and other artists. Perugino was buried in the
church but we don't know the exact spot. (The church does not
have an appropriate bell-tower).

Returning to the square, on the left is the Archeological *Museum*
Because of the serious damage caused by the flood, the rooms on
the ground floor are still in restoration. The building in which the
museum is located is called "of the crocetta" because it is in the
form of a cross. The entrance is on Via della Colonna past the
garden, enclosed by the fence. This Museum is considered one of
the most important in the world for Etruscan art and sculture
Among the most important works we mention: in the large room
of the first floor, the *Chimera* (fig. 174) from Arezzo in bronze (V
cent. BC); the "Arringatore" (haranguer) (III-II cent. BC); "Ido
lino", bronze Greek sculpture (second half V cent.). Among the
numerous works on the second floor is the famous *Françoise Vase*
of Etrusco-Italic origin.

In the rooms of the first floor, on the left, is the very important
Egyptian Museum.

SIXTH ITINERARY

Church of S. Maria Novella – Via dei Fossi – Piazza Goldoni – Via della Vigna Nuova – Palazzo Rucellai – Church of Ognissanti – Lungarno and Ponte Vespucci – Ponte alla Carraia – Lungarno and Corsini Palace – Ponte and Church of St. Trinità – Church of SS. Apostoli – Palace of the Parte Guelfa – Davanzati Palace – Strozzi Palace. (Map of the monuments nos. 1, 27, 28, 30, 31, 32 and 33).

CHURCH OF SANTA MARIA NOVELLA

It was begun in 1278 by the Dominican Friars Sisto and Ristoro and was finished in 1360. The beautiful bell-tower is by Fra Jacopo Talenti and helpers in Lombard style with several stories decorated with small arches and harmonious mullioned windows.

Façade (fig. 175). The façade was built around 1300 with green and white marble and harmonizes well with the architectural complex of the Church. While the lower part is in Gothic style with Romanesque traces (the blind arches were inspired by the Baptistry), the beautiful *portal* and upper part were designed by Alberti (1456) in the Renaissance period. The two *astronomical instruments* at the

Fig. 175 - Square and Church of Santa Maria Novella

PLAN OF THE CHURCH OF S. MARIA NOVELLA

1. Tomb of Senator Ippolito Venturi (S Rissi).
2. Monument to the Blessed Villana (Bernardo Rossellino).
3. Presentation in the Temple (Naldini, 1577).
4. Deposition (Naldini).
5. S. Vincent Ferrari Preaching (Iacopo del Meglio - XVI cent.).
6. St. Raymond raising a dead child (Iacopo Ligozzi).
7. Della Pura Chapel.
8. Rucellai Chapel.
9. Bardi Chapel.
10. Strozzi Chapel.
11. High Altar.
12. Gondi Chapel.
13. Gaddi Chapel.
14. Strozzi Chapel.
15. Sacristy.
16. St. Hyacinth (A. Allori).
17. St. Catherine of Siena (Poccetti).
18. Resurrection (Vasari).
19. Annunciation (Santi di Tito).
20. Samaritan at the well (Alessandro Allori).
21. Resurrection of Lazzarus (Santi di Tito).

A. Entrance to the Cloisters.
B. Chiostro Verde (Green Cloister).
C. Ante-refectory.
D. Refectory.
E. Spanish Chapel.
F. Cloister of the Dead.
G. Old Cemetery.

right and left, are by Ignazio Danti (1512), the court astronomer of Cosimo I. On the right side is the old *Cemetery* of the Noble families (enclosed by the portico) that gives its name to the small street (via degli Avelli).

Interior. It is in the form of a "T" with three naves and a cross vaulted ceiling. The length is 99 meters, width 28 meters and width of the transept 61 meters.

The clustered columns are more closely spaced at the front, creating a major perspective effect. Fortunately the Church did not suffer the unhappy alterations of Santa Croce: here Vasari limited himself to modifying the center of the nave and adding the lateral altars. Among the most notable works we mention, at beginning of the right nave: *Monument to the Blessed Villana,* by Bernardo Rossellino and helpers (1415).

Observe, on the pillar of the central nave to the left: *Pulpit* with the spiral staircase, by Buggiano, following a design by Brunelleschi, with low-reliefs representing *Stories of the Virgin.*

Behind the pulpit, on the wall of the left nave, fresco (restored) by Masaccio (1427) of the *Trinity with Mary and St. John*; below the portraits of the donors kneeling. In the false high relief is the skeleton (death) with an iscription.

High Altar. The beautiful stained glass windows are of the XV cent. The altar of polychrome marble (added in the XVII cent.) alters the atmosphere and has a *candelabrum* of the XV century. If there is no religious function in course, from the apse we can better admire the famous frescoes in which Domenico Ghirlandaio (1485-90), aided by his many collaborators and students, among whom was a young Michelangelo, painted the most faithful documentation of the private life of the wealthy XV century Florentine society. In the *scenes of the Virgin and St. John the Baptist* (fig. 176) women and girls are shown with their typical hairdos and many famous Florentine personages are represented in the costumes of the time. On the lower central wall is a portrait of the donor *Giovanni Tornabuoni* and his wife Francesca Pitti. In the vault are *large figures of the Evangelists.* Following, on the right, is the STROZZI CHAPEL with frescoes by Filippino Lippi (1502), representing the *Miracles of the Apostles Philip and John.* Behind the altar, *tomb of Filippo Strozzi,* a masterpiece by Benedetto da Maiano (1491-93).

Observe, on the wall in front of this Chapel, among other works, terra-cotta bust of *St. Antonino,* of the XV cent. *Above is a Gothic tomb of Todice Aliotti,* Bishop of Fiesole, who died in 1436, by Tino da Camaino. Below, on the left, *tomb of Joseph, Patriarch of*

Fig. 176 - St. Maria Novella - Main Chapel - Domenico Ghirlandaio: Scenes of the Madonna

203

Fig. 177 - Basilica of St. Maria Novella - Spanish Chapel - Andrea da Firen
Central and right walls

Constantinople, who died in this convent during the Council of Florence of 1439, that unified the Greek and Roman Churches. Ending the transept is the raised RUCELLAI CHAPEL with XIV cent frescoes. In the floor is the *memorial figure of the Domenican* Leonardo Dati, by Ghiberti (1452), at one time in front of the main altar. On the left: BARDI CHAPEL or of the *Sacrament* with XIV cent. frescoes attributed to the Bolognese painter Lippo Dalmasio. Returning to the transept, on the left is the GONDI CHAPEL built by Giuliano da Sangallo (1503) with polychrome marble. On the altar is the celebrated Crucifix by Brunelleschi. In the vault, the deteriorated frescoes were perhaps done by Greek artists who worked in Florence in the XIII century.

GADDI CHAPEL. Architectural decoration by Giovanni Antonio Dosio (1575-77); in the vault, frescoes and stuccoes are by Alessandro Allori. On the altar is a table by Bronzino, *Jesus resuscitating the daughter of Jairus.*

From here we climb to the CHAPEL OF THE STROZZI OF MANTUA, entirely frescoed by Nardo di Cione (XIV cent.). On the back wall, the *Final Judgement*; on the left, *Paradise* inspired by Dante's Divine Comedy, who is represented among the *elect*. On the right wall, the *circles of Hell.* (These famous frescoes might be missing because of restoration). On the altar, the altar-piece signed and dated 1357, is by Andrea di Cione called Orcagna, Nardo's brother. At the foot of the stairs, on the right we enter (if open), the beautiful *Sacristy* by Fra Jacopo Talenti (1350), the architect of the bell-tower. It contains the beautiful *lavabo* of marble and glazed terra cotta by Giovanni Della Robbia, above is a *Crucifix* by Giotto.

The large wardrobes are of the XVII century. Heading towards the exit, observe, on the interior façade of the Church, the large stained glass *rose window* with the *Incoronation of the Virgin*, believed to be designed by Botticelli.

The *Nativity* in the lunette is in mosaic of the XV century.

Below, on the right wall, *Annunciation*, *Nativity*, *Epiphany* and *Baptism*, XIV century Florentine frescoes. Leaving the church, on the right is the entrance to the

Green Cloister (Chiostro Verde). So-called because of the colors of the famous frescoes on the walls that were removed for restoration having been damaged by the weather. They are now on display in the Refectory where they can be seen by asking the custodian. They represent: *Scenes from the Old Testament*, among which we mention the *Deluge* and *Drunkenness of Noah*, by Paolo Uccello who was the first artist to seriously study the laws of volumetric movement n perspective. Under the portico, opposite to the entrance on the left, a beautiful portal, flanked by two wide mullioned windows with twisted columns, leads to the famous SPANISH CHAPEL (fig. 177).

SPANISH CHAPEL

It is a splendid architectural creation of Jacopo Talenti (c. 1350), and served as the Chapter room of the Convent, later for the religious functions of the Spanish members at the court of Eleanor of Toledo, wife of Cosimo I. On the walls and in the vault of this splendid Chapel, we can admire the famous cycle of frescoes by Andrea Bonaiuti, called da Firenze (c. 1355) representing the allegorical theme of *True Penitence*, taken from a poem by Passanti (1298-1358). On the left wall, *Triumph of St. Thomas Aquinas.* On the right wall: *Activity and Triumph of the Dominicans*: on the left, the *civil authorities dominated by mortals*; in the background is the *cupola of the Cathedral*, as projected by the XIV cent. artist. Observe on the right wall the black and white dogs (Domini canes— dogs of God) who defend the flock of christians from the wolves (heretics). Above St. Dominic, St. Thomas and St. Peter Martyr confuting the heretics. Youth is represented by Dames and cavaliers who waste their lives in wordly passtimes; a Dominican confesses and absolved a penitent. Still higher, St. Dominic indicates the way to Paradise, St. Peter welcomes the faithful who are crowned by two angels.

Returning to the Cloister, farther ahead on the left, is a SECOND SMALL CLOISTER. At one time it was the cemetary of the great families, with XIV century frescoes and a *Noli me tangere* in terracotta, by Della Robbia.

Returning to the square observe the two marble obelisks, with four bronze turtles at the base by Giambologna (1608). The obelisks served to mark the limits during the "Palio" (coach races) that were held here from 1563. On the opposite side of the square is the LOGGIA OF SAN PAOLO (1489-96), inspired by Brunelleschi's portico in Piazza SS. Annunziata. On the front are nine terracotta medallions by Giovanni, the last of the Della Robbia. In the first medallion on the left is a *self-portrait of Andrea Della Robbia* who portrayed his uncle Luca on the extreme right. In the lunette under the portico, *Meeting of St. Francis and St. Dominic*, a masterpiece by Andrea Della Robbia. On the corner of via della Scala, *Tabernacle with Madonna and Saints*, by Francesco d'Antonio, the original of which was removed and replaced by a copy (c. 1425). Walking around the square, on the side near via delle Belle Donne, we can better admire the Church which Michelangelo used to call "my bride". Returning near to the portico of San Paolo is the via dei Fossi, on which are many antique shops, leading to Piazzetta Goldoni, with a *statue of the Venetian Poet* by Cambi (1873). On the left is via Vigna Nuova where, at N. 18, we can admire the beautiful *Rucellai palace.*

Rucellai Palace. Built on a design by Leon Battista Alberti who, inspired by antiquity, is stylistically opposite to Brunelleschi. Observe the exquisite pilasters of the doric, ionic and corinthian orders and the regular flat blocks which render the façade harmonious and linear, rather than plastic. The beautiful mullioned windows are of a traditional character. Opposite the palace is the *Loggia Rucellai* attributed to Alberti, that has been brought back to its original aspect after having been walled up in the XVII century.

Returning to Piazzetta Goldoni we continue along Borgo Ognissanti where, farther ahead, is the Hospital of St. Giovanni di Dio, which occupies the old houses of the Vespucci where Amerigo Vespucci was born. (He is buried in Avila, Spain).

PIAZZA OGNISSANTI

Facing the square are the two large Excelsior and Grand Hotels. In the center, the modern bronze group of *Hercules fighting the Lion* is by Romano Romanelli. On the corner of Borgognissanti, Lensi Busini Palace later Quaratesi, with XV century graffitti decoration. now seat of the French Institute.

CHURCH OF OGNISSANTI

Founded in the XIII century, it was entirely reconstructed in the XVIII century. Above the door, the lunette in glazed terra-cotta showing the *Incoronation of the Virgin* is attributed to Benedetto Buglioni. The beautiful Romanesque bell-tower is of the XIII cent.

Interior. Seventeenth century style with a single nave and a transept. Beginning on the right wall: the second altar, frescoes by Domenico and David Ghirlandaio (c. 1470); above, *Madonna of Mercy who gathers the Vespucci family under her mantle.*

Ahead, between the third and fourth altar, *St. Augustine in his Study*, frescoe by Botticelli (1480). Followed by a XVI century *pulpit* with marble bas-reliefs of *Stories of St. Francis.*

Turning in the right transept and entering the chapel on the right, we see on the floor, the marble disc marking the spot where Botticelli was buried.

High Altar. In the cupola, *Glory of Paradise*, fresco by Giovanni da San Giovanni (1616-17). Heading towards the door notice on the wall between the fourth and third altars, *St. Jerome in his study*

Fig. 178 - Refectory of Ognissanti - Domenico Ghirlandaio: Last Supper (detail)

209

by Domenico Ghirlandaio (1480); it is interesting to confront it with Botticelli's on the opposite wall, which is psychologically more vibrant. Leaving the Church, if you ring the bell on the right, you may visit the picturesque Cloister of the Convent, in the style of Michelozzo, with frescoes by Florentine artists of the XVII century. In the back, to the left, is the entrance to the Refectory with Domenico Ghirlandaio's *Last Supper* (1480) which was admired by Leonardo (fig. 178). proceeding to the river, on the right, notice the

Ponte Vespucci. Built after the last war with contributions from the Latin Nations. Continuing along the Arno we can admire the scenery offered by the hillside of Bellosguardo and the cupola of the Seminary of Cestello in front of us. In the distance Michelangelo Square and San Miniato. Walking left on Lungarno we reach the Ponte alla Carraia, destroyed by the German mines (1944) rebuilt in its original style.

After the bridge begins Lungarno Corsini; on the corner of Piazzetta Goldoni is the RICASOLI PALACE, attributed to Michelozzo. Ahead is the CORSINI PALACE, by Silvani and Antonio Ferri (XVII cent.), with the beautiful courtyard and lateral wings that, because of its rational elegance, inspired other residential palaces in Europe. On the first floor of the Palace is the *Art Gallery*, considered one of the most important private Galleries and containing works by Signorelli, Raphael and other famous artists. For the visit consult the doorman. On the ground floor is the seat of the cultural society "Leonardo da Vinci". The Corsini family had some important historical figures among its members like, Andrea, bishop of Fiesole (XIV cent.) and Lorenzo later Pope Clement XII. Farther ahead an epigraph recalls where the houses of the Compagni were, the family to which the historian Dino Compagni, contemporary of Dante, belonged. At N. 4 is PALAZZO GIANFIGLIAZZI, a Renaissance building modified in the last century; an epigraph recalls that Manzoni stayed here in 1872. At n. 2 another epigraph marks where Vittorio Alfieri died in 1803.

Ponte Santa Trinita (fig. 179). This jewel of Italian architecture by Ammannati (1570), consists of three wide arches sustained by enormous pillars. Destroyed in the last war, it was rebuilt by the Florentines exactly as it had been and where it had been, using the original stones recuperated in the river. The four statues that decorate the corners are *Summer* and *Autumn* by Caccini, *Winter* by Landini, and *Spring* by Francavilla. These statues fell into the river because of the mine explosions and recuperated, they were put back in their original positions. The head of Spring was again lost and an American newspaper offered generous reward for its finding. In 1961, dur-

Figs. 179-180 - Bridge of Santa Trinità and Square of Santa Trinità

Fig. 180 bis - Basilica of Santa Trinità - Domenico Ghirlandaio: St. Francis resuscitates a child

ing some works in the river, the head was found by a Town employee, much to the joy of the Florentines who had given it up for lost or stolen during the war.

On the left of the bridge is the SPINI-FERRONI PALACE (1298), perfect example of a typical wealthy medieval home, three stories high with a crenellated top.

PIAZZA SANTA TRINITÀ

In the small square (fig. 180), the tall *granite column* is originally from the Baths of Caracalla, donated by Pius IV to Cosimo I, who had it placed here to commemorate the victory of Montemurlo (1537). The porphyry statue of "Justice" on the top of the column is by Tadda (1581). The bronze metal was added later. On the right of the square, is the beautiful BARTOLINI-SALIMBENI PALACE by Baccio d'Agnolo, who began with this palace a new style of homes for the rich. The criticism of his fellow citizens prompted him to engrave over the door: "carpere promptius quam imitari", that is, "to criticize is easier than to imitate".

CHURCH OF SANTA TRINITÀ

Considered one of the oldest churches of the city, it is in Florentine

Gothic style. Built by the Vallombrosian monks in the XI cent., it was rebuilt in the XII cent. and enlarged in the following century. The late Renaissance façade is by Buontalenti (1593-94). The statue of *St. Alexis* on the left, and the relief on the central door representing the *Trinity* are by Caccini.

Interior. It has three naves with pointed arches and cross vaults. The chapels were added in the XIV century. On the interior façade can be seen remains of the original Romanesque church; the fresco of the *Trinity* is of the late XIV century.

Among the important works we mention: the fourth chapel of the right nave (Bartolini Chapel), frescoed by the late-Gothic painter Lorenzo Monaco (teacher of Beato Angelico), who represented *Stories of Mary* and *figures of the Prophets* in the vault; on the altar the Annunciation. In the right tansept on the tall column, *statue of David*; in the lunette, *Sibilla Tiburtina that announces the birth of the Savior to Augustus*, by Domenico Ghirlandaio (1483). By the same artist we admire in the Sassetti Chapel (the light switch is on the left): *Stories and miracles* of *St. Francis* (fig. 181), among these: *St. Francis resuscitates a child* (fig. 180 bis); above, portrait of *Politian* with *Lorenzo the Magnificent and his children* shown in a typical Florentine background with the personages wearing costumes and hairdos of the times. In the frescoes we can see the *Spini Palace*, *Ponte St. Trinità* and the *Loggia* in *Signoria Square*. Below, on the sides, *Tombs of Francesco Sassetti* and his *wife Nera Corsi*, the donors of the *Chapel*, shown in prayer. On the altar, *Adoration of the Shepherds*, also by Ghirlandaio, inspired by the "Triptych" of Hugo Van der Goes in the Uffizi Gallery. The following Chapel contains the miraculous *Crucifix* of *St. Giovanni* Gualberti (generally covered), founder of the Vallombrosian order (XI cent.). According to legend, this Crucifix bent its head in a sign of approval because St. Giovanni pardoned his brother's murderer.

High Altar. On the altar is a triptych with *Trinity and Saints* by Mariotto di Nardo (1416). In the vault and in the lunettes, the frescoes (unfortunately deteriorated) are by Alessio Baldovinetti (c. 1471), with the *Patriarchs*, *Sacrifice of Isaac* and *Moses receiving the tables of the law*. In the second chapel (on the left of the High Altar), famous *tomb of Bishop Benozzo Federighi*, rare marble sculpture by Luca Della Robbia (1454-56), with a frieze in polychrome terracotta. In the fifth chapel of the left nave, *wooden statue* of *Mary Magdalen* by Desiderio da Settignano and Benedetto da Maiano, inspired, it is believed, by Donatello's Magdalen. In the central nave, the stairs leads down to the *Romanesque Crypt*, that conserves some elements of the primitive church. (Turn on light if necessary). Returning to the Piazza St. Trinità, observe the elegant via Tornabuoni, known for its famous palaces, its book stores and elegant stores. The first circle of walls surrounding Florence were here and continued on Borgo SS. Apostoli out to the Ponte Vecchio. The brief walk on the right, gives us a chance to admire one of the sections of the city that best conserves its old aspect and leads us to the Church of SS. Apostoli.

CHURCH OF SS. APOSTOLI

The Church (generally opened in the morning) was built in the XI century but was remodelled in the XV and XVI centuries. After some opportune restorations it has once again acquired its original aspect. The Beautiful *Portal* is attributed to Benedetto da Rovezzano.

Interior. Has three naves divided by columns, with a semicircular apse. It is a splendid example of Florentine-Romanesque architecture, like the Baptistry and San Miniato. The classic proportions of this church certainly influenced the Renaissance buildings designed by Brunelleschi. In the Church are conserved some stone splinters from the Holy Sepulchre which are used as a flint to light the fire-works in the XVII century cart during the "Scoppio del Carro" on Easter Sunday, in front of the Baptistry. On the left of the apse, terracotta *tabernacle* by Giovanni Della Robbia, and *Tomb of Oddo Altoviti* by Benedetto da Rovezzano. Leaving the Church, farther ahead, observe the Medieval "tower-houses". On the right "Roselli Del Turco Palace" by Baccio d'Agnolo (early XVI cent.). On the left is the narrow via del Fiordaliso, with interesting medieval houses whose upper stories jut out and rest on corbels.

Continuing on Borgo SS. Apostoli, at N. 8, on the left, remains of the houses of the Buondelmonti, which were destroyed in the tumult of the "Ciompi" in 1378. The remains were included into the building of the Certosini. According to Legend, the origins of the struggles between Guelphs and Ghibellines in Florence, begin with the slaying of Buondelmonte dei Buondelmonti (Easter 1215). Farther ahead is the central via Por Santa Maria. On the left, via delle Terme with its old tower-houses. Nearby the building of the "Borsa Merci" (Stock market) was built after the last war, but it unfortunately covers the old palace of the "Parte Guelfa". On the left of the Palace of Parte Guelfa is the small, narrow via del Capaccio, with its beautiful XV cent. Cenacci Palace with graffiti decoration and its splendid loggia.

On the right is the Palazzo dei Capitani di Parte Guelfa.

Fig. 181 - Basilica of Santa Trinità - Domenico Ghirlandaio: Approval of the order of St. Francis

PALAZZO DEI CAPITANI DI PARTE GUELFA

Splendid XIV cent. building with wide mullioned windows, decorated with crests below the embattlements. The picturesque covered staircase ith small octagonal columns leads to the first floor, where Brunelleschi built the large Renaissance hall with smooth walls and large windows, that faces via delle Terme and via Capaccio. The staircase on the via Capaccio was added by Vasari. In the large hall with the beautiful wooden ceiling, enriched by works of Luca Della Robbia, cultural conferences and political meetings are held. On the left of the open stairs is the ex church of San Biagio, now the seat of the "Università Popolare" (University of the People), with its famous Library.

Continuing on the left, on via Porta Rossa, we come to the medieval Piazza Davanzati with its cut down tower-house. On the left is the Davizzi-Davanzati Palace.

DAVIZZI-DAVANZATI PALACE

It is of the XIV cent. with the "Loggia"added in the XV century, it is now a Museum. A visit is particularly recommended since it is the only example of a XV cent. Florentine-home, reorganized with furniture copied from the originals now in the Museum of Philadelphia. From here we can admire the old Torrigiani Palace of the XIV (now the Hotel Porta Rossa). Continuing on the right, in Piazza Davanzati behind the Central Post Office, is via Sassetti where the remains of some old palaces can be seen. On the left is Piazza Strozzi with the Odeon Cinema, which is located in the "Strozzino", begun by Michelozzo (1458), continued by Giuliano da Sangallo (1460-65). On the right is the Strozzi Palace.

STROZZI PALACE

Begun by Benedetto da Maiano (fig. 182), for Filippo Strozzi, an unfortunate rival of the Medici. It is a splendid example of civil architecture with its rusticated stone, inspired by the Medici-Riccardi Palace, but with more harmonious proportions. The *palace* has beautiful mullioned windows and a magnificent cornice, typical of the Florentine palaces of the time, left incomplete by Cronaca, who continued the construction of the palace until 1507. Also by Cronaca is the beautiful courtyard, inspired by Michelozzo. The famous wrought-iron lanterns that decorate the corners of the palace exterior, are by the bizarre and able artesan, Caparra. To-day the palace is used for international exposition like the annual Antique Show, the

Italian High Fashion shows and other cultural and artistic manifestation. Here also is the seat of the "Center of Renaissance Studies" and the noted "Gabinetto Vieusseux", with the Library and reading-room.

Fig. 182 - Strozzi Palace

FIRST EXCURSION

Viale dei Colli (Avenue of the Hills) – *Piazzale Michelangelo – Church of San Miniato.* (South of the city – Monumental plan Nos. 24 and 35 – Bus N. 13).

These winding avenues, that are a continuation of those surrounding the city, below, are called "of the hills", because they were built on the green picturesque hillside by the Florentine Architect Giuseppe Poggi.

If one goes to Piazzale Michelangelo by bus and wishes to continue down the entire length of the avenue, he must be careful to take the bus that continues in the same direction, since there are two buses which travel in opposite directions and are distinguished by the colors. N. 13 red or black.

PIAZZALE MICHELANGELO

It is world renowned as one of the most panoramic sites of Italy (fig. 183). Superb is the view of the city and the hills of Fiesole enjoyed from this spot. Looking down we can admire the various bridges and the Arno which flows towards Pisa, flanked in the distance by the famous Cascine Park. To the left of the Piazzale, are the picturesque walls of San Giorgio and the Fortress Belvedere. Standing with one's back to the city, to the left of the Square, on high, is the Church of San Miniato; on the right, in the distance, the Castle of *Torre del Gallo.* In the center of the Piazzale is a bronze copy of Michelangelo's David and bronze copies of his statues of *Night, Day, Dusk* and *Dawn,* the originals of which are in the Medici Chapels. Moving towards the left at the end of the square, observe the picturesque stairs, called "Monte alle Croci" (Hill of the Crosses) because of the symbolic stations of the Cross, that lead to the Franciscan *Church of S. Salvatore al Monte,* rebuilt in the XVI century following a design by Cronaca. Higher up, to the right, is the *Church of San Miniato al Monte.*

CHURCH OF SAN MINIATO AL MONTE

It is inserted between the beautiful Bishop's palace (1296-1320) (now inhabited by the monks of Monte Oliveto), on the right, and, on the left, the remains of the old bastions, with the *bell-Tower* by Baccio d'Agnolo damaged during the famous seige of 1530, which saw Michelangelo as the engineer of the Florentine fortifications. The façade of the Church is strictly Florentine Romanesque style with green and white marble. In the tympanum is a XII cent. mosaic representing *Christ between the Madonna and San Miniato* (fig. 185). The Church (fig. 184), was built in the XI century on the old Oratory (erected by San Miniato the first Florentine Christian martyr), and is the most notable example of Florentine Romanesque architecture.

Fig. 183 - Piazzale Michelangelo - View of the city
Fig. 184 - Basilica of San Miniato al Monte

Fig. 185 · Basilica of San Miniato · Christ blessing (mosaic)

Interior (fig. 186). It is divided into three naves. The wall structure is intact but the decorative part underwent restorations (the roof, columns and lateral walls). The beautiful floor of the central nave is richly decorated with inlaid marble Symbols of the Zodiac, among which are lions, doves and other symbols (1207). In the center of the Church is the small but splendid marble Renaissance Chapel by Michelozzo (1442) built to house the *Crucifix of St. Giovanni Gualberto* (now conserved in the Church of St. Trinità). The altar-piece by Agnolo Gaddi represents *Episodes of Saint Miniato and St. Giovanni Gualberto*, the *Annunciation* and *Stories of the Passion*. The Chapel is enriched by small Corinthian columns and pilasters, and the barrel vaulted roof decorated in terra-cotta by Luca Della Robbia, and the motto "Semper" by the donor, Piero dei Medici.

Right nave. Old frescoes; among the most notable, *Madonna and Saints* by Paolo Schiavo (1439). In the Crypt, with a cross vaulted ceiling sustained by slender columns, are the remains of San Miniato.

Chancel. Raised and enclosed by a splendid balustrade decorated with inlaid green and white marble rosettes. The famous *pulpit* (1207) is the most notable work XIII century Florentine sculpture. The exquisite inlaid wood stalls are by Giovanni da Gaiole and Francesco

220

Fig. 186 - Basilica of San Miniato - Interior - Luca della Robbia: Tabernacle di Domenico (1470). Farther ahead on the right, is the Sacristy with frescoes by Spinello Aretino (1387) showing *Stories and Miracle of St. Benedict*.

From the chancel observe the semi-circular apse, with arches and columns of black and white marble and graceful capitals; the large mosaic (1279) (restored) with *Christ between the Madonna and St. Miniato crowned* (because he was of Imperial origin). At the base of the mosaic are symbols of the Evangelists. If one is here during the morning when the sun's rays penetrate the windows of the apse closed with translucent marble slabs, he will see how the soft light discretely illuminates the Church. By ringing the bell at the door it is possible to visit the beautiful cloister and the splendid hall of the Bishop's Palace. Descending once again to the church, on the right is the Chapel of the Cardinal of Portugal.

Chapel of the Cardinal of Portugal. It was built by Antonio Manetti, pupil of Brunelleschi (1459-66), for Jacopo di Lusitania, Archbishop of Lisbon, nephew of King Alfonso of Portugal, and is a strictly Renaissance work. In the vault are five *medallions* by Luca Della Robbia representing the *Holy Spirit* and the *Cardinal Virtues* (1416-66). Against the right wall is the famous *Tomb* of the *Cardinal of Portugal*, masterpiece by Antonio Rossellino. On the altar, the painting of *St. Vincent, St. James* and *St. Eustachius* is a copy of the original by Antonio and Piero Pollaiolo, now in the Uffizi. On the left, *Bishop's chair*, and above, *Annunciation* frescoed by Baldovinetti (1466-67). The two Flying *Angels* are by Antonio del Pollaiolo.

Heading towards the exit, on the right is the *Porta Santa* (Holy Door) so-called because, according to legend, remains of Christian martyrs were found here; on the left is the Tomb of Giuseppe Giusti. Returning to the square in front of the church, we see the Monumental Cemetery.

Monumental Cemetery. Called of the "Porte Sante", designed by the architect Matas (1839), where many famous persons are buried including Carlo Lorenzini (Collodi), Stibbert, Temple-Leader, Villari, Salvemini and others.

SECOND EXCURSION

San Domenico - Fiesole. (North of the city. Monumental map N. 38 and 39. Bus service N. 7 from Piazza San Marco. It is about 6 Km. from the center of Florence. Altitude 320 meters).

For those using private cars the usual route goes from Piazza del Duomo to Piazza Libertà. In this square is one of the oldest gates of the city: *Porta S. Gallo* (1284 - plan N. 36). In front of this, the Baroque arch is by Jadod (1745) and was erected for the entrance in Florence of Francesco of Lorraine, the successor of the Medici. Turning right on viale Matteotti we reach the *English Protestant Cemetery* (plan N. 37) where, among others, the poet Arthur High Clough (d. 1861) and Elisabeth Barret Browning (d. 1863), are buried. Following the signs for Fiesole, we cross a bridge over the railroad and take the third street on the right, viale Alessandro Volta which leads to the picturesque section called San Domenico which takes its name from the convent (fig. 187).

CONVENT OF SAN DOMENICO

Built in the XV century. Here the twenty year old Beato Angelico became a Dominican monk. The Church was remodelled in the XVII century by Nigetti and contains, among other interesting works, a

Fig. 187 - Hills of Fiesole

Madonna and Child with Saints by Angelico (in the second chapel). There are numerous historical villas in San Domenico, including the "Villa Sparta", on the right of the convent; farther up, surrounded by cypress trees, the "Villa Papiniano"; at the top in a dominating position, painted yellow, is the "Medici Villa" that was a cultural center under Lorenzo the Magnificent. After San Domenico, on the right, the road winds higher between villas with beautiful gardens, olive groves and tall cypresses, making this a landscape of great harmony between nature and man made works.

The high hill on the right is Monte Ceceri, from where Leonardo tried out his first experimental flights. At the last curve near Fiesole is the entrance to the Medici Villa with its splendid park. On the right side are remains of the Etruscan walls.

FIESOLE

An old Etruscan city, it held a notable position during the Roman era, especially under the Empire. The archeological zone mentioned later is testimony to the importance of this old city. In Mino da Fiesole Square (fig. 188) is the Cathedral. On the left of the Archbishop's Palace is the large Seminary. On the right of the Square

Fig. 188 - Fiesole - Piazza Mino and Cathedral

the bronze equestrian monuments of *Vittorio Emanuele II* and *Garibaldi* are by Calzolari (1906), recalling their meeting at Teano. Behind is the old Municipal building (restored), with crests of the mayors. On the right, *Church of St. Maria Primerana* with its XVII century façade.

Cathedral, dedicated to St. Romulus. It was begun in 1028 and covered with the local stone.

Interior is Romanesque, divided into three naves, with arches sustained by solid stone columns and splendid capitals. As in S. Miniato, here the chancel is raised and, in the first chapel on the right, is the famous *Tomb of Bishop Salutati* by Mino da Fiesole (1466), who sculpted the *bust of the Bishop,* one of his most vibrant works. In the next chapel is an old copy of the *Martyrdom of St. Romulus* in which we see Fiesole as it was at the time. On the *high altar*, the triptych with the *Madonna, Child and Saints* is by Bicci di Lorenzo (1440). In the apse are XVI cent. frescoes with Stories *of St. Romulus.* In the church observe the XV cent. pulpit that inspired Brunelleschi for the one in Santa Maria Novella. Returning to the square behind the apse of the Cathedral is the entrance to the Roman Theatre.

ROMAN THEATRE AND ARCHEOLOGICAL ZONE

After admiring the solemn scenery that encloses such great testimony of the past, on the right we enter the *Tempietto*, in Ionic style, by Ezio Cerpi (1912-14), which is a small Museum containing archeological objects found in the Fiesole area. Among these is the statuette of Etruscan-ionic art representing *Hercules* (VI cent. BC); the Etruscan mirror with the *Sacrifice of Polixena*, the head of the statue of Claudius. (The Museum is in the process of reordination.) Leaving the Museum, below right is the Roman Theatre (fig. 189).

Roman Theatre. It is Greek style, was discovered in 1809 and excavated by Gamurrini (1873). It dates back to Silla, was enriched in the I and II centuries A.D., and was enlarged during Hadrian's era. Heading down towards the west, we see two sacrificial altars from Etruscan times. On the left is an Etrusco-Roman Temple, of which the entrance, steps are conserved. On the right of the Temple the remains of an Etruscan gate are visible, with parts of the Etruscan wall, built with colossal blocks, that extends east to the Baths. Leaving the Roman Theatre, on the right is the BANDINI MUSEUM.

Fig. 189 - Fiesole - Roman Theater

BANDINI MUSEUM

On the ground floor are some terra-cotta works; on the first floor in the first room, works by Bicci di Lorenzo, Agnolo and Taddeo Gaddi and other artists identified in the pamphlets available to the visitors. In the second room we can admire works by Botticelli, Filippo Lippi, the famous *Triumphs of Religion, Love, Chastity* and *Time*, by Jacopo del Sellaio. After visiting this small but important Museum, if one has time, we suggest walking down to the left on the picturesque road bordered by cypress trees that, winding upward, reaches the *Franciscan Monastery*, passing by the *Monumental Cemetery* where the sculptore Duprè (d. 1882) is buried. Here is this artist's famous *Deposition*. If one's time is limited, then return to the main square (Mino da Fiesole), from where he can directly climb via S. Francesco, located between the *Seminary* and the *Bishop's Palace*. Continuing on high to the right, is the entrance to the small Park from where we can admire the Archeological Zone below and the surrounding hills.

Leaving the park, on the left, we enter the beautiful panoramic garden, in which there is a *Monument to the War Dead* and a splendid view of the city. From here we arrive at the vast panoramic terrace where, at one time, the old Etruscan walls were found. Opposite, in the beautiful square where the panorama is more ample, is the Basilica of St. Alexander, bishop of the city. This V century church was erected on an Etruscan temple and was renovated and restored in later times. Higher up, we visit the Convent of San Francesco (figs. 190-191).

CONVENT OF SAN FRANCESCO

In 1330 it was the Oratory of the "Romite Fiorentine". In 1407, the Monastery passed to the Franciscans, who enlarged it in the successive eras. The graceful Church has a simple vault. Among the most important works, behind the beautiful grating, *Annunciation* attributed to Raffaellino del Garbo. The *inlaid stalls* of the choir are of the XV cent., the Renaissance arch is attributed to Benedetto da Maiano. On the left, is the entrance to the Sacristy.

Sacristy. Modernized and has frescoes by Baccio M. Bacci. From the graceful *Cloister* we descend to the MISSION MUSEUM. From the balconi we can admire a panorama of Florence, the Cascine Park, which appears as a dark strip, and the Arno which flows towards Pisa. Leaving the Convent, on the left is the entrance to the picturesque MEDIEVAL CLOISTER. The small stair-case leads to the severe cells of the Monastery, where St. Bernardine of Siena lived when he was the Superior of the Convent. If the visitor happens to be here at dusk, he will never forget the vast view of Florence, surrounded by her splendid hills.

Returning to the square, the bus leaves for the city. If one has a car, when arriving at S. Domenico, we suggest taking via Boccaccio on the right, where, after the narrow curves, on the right is the Villa Schifanois with its graceful garden. It was donated by Myron Taylor to the Vatican (where he was ambassador), and is now the seat of the Pious XII Institute, directed by American Sisters, and frequented by girls studying music, humanities, fine arts and Italian.

Ahead, on the left, is the vast splendid garden of the Villa Palmieri where Boccaccio, taking refuge here from the plague of 1348, is said to have written his Decameron. This historic villa, that hosted Queen Victoria of England in 1888 and famous writers, is now owned by the Committee for the conservation of historic villas.

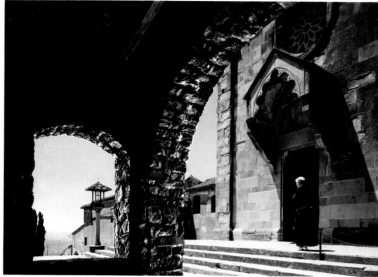

Figs. 190-191 - Fiesole - St. Francis - The Church

Museums less frequented, that merit being visited.

(Because of flood damage, some of these museums might still be in restoration).

Bardini Museum. Located on the right of Ponte alle Grazie, in Piazza dei Mozzi (monumental plan N. 20), in front of the XVI century Palaces of the Torrigiani, by Baccio d'Agnolo. The XIX century Palace, willed to the city in 1923 with all its art treasures by the antique dealer Bardini, contains, in the large rooms of its two stories, a beautiful *Venetian ceiling*, paintings, tapestries, ceramics and other numerous objects of art.

Museum of the "Horne Foundation". It is located on Via dei Benci (near S. Croce) on the right of the picturesque Piazza delle Colonnine, so-called because of the small *loggia* supported by two columns of the Alberti tower-house. It was donated in 1916 to the city of Florence by the writer and collector Herbert P. Horne. The building, formerly of the Alberti then of the Corsi families, is attributed to Giuliano da Sangallo, who executed the beautiful *courtyard*, probably in collaboration with Andrea Sansovino. Other than the library, numerous works of art are displayed by artists such as: Simone Martini, Bernardo Daddi, Dosso Dossi, Filippino Lippi, Salvator Rosa and many others.

National Museum of Science. Situated in the Palace in Piazza Castellani, on the left side of the Uffizi. A severe three story building with solid round arched windows, and made of rusticated stone, from 1574 to 1841, it was the seat of the Justices of the "Rota". Restored from 1888 to 1930, it became the seat of the only Scientific Museum in Italy, and later the seat of the Accademy of the "Crusca", for the study of the Italian language. Among the numerous and important instruments from the Medici collections and private gifts, are rare instruments invented by Galileo Galilei.

Museum of Anthropology and Ethnology. Founded by Mantegazza (1869), it is located in the Palazzo Non Finito (unfinished Palace - on via del Proconsolo 12), so-called because it was left unfinished by Buontalenti who began its construction in 1593 for Alessandro Strozzi.

Museum of Zoology called "La Specola" (observatory). Grand duke Pietro Leopoldo (1779) bought the old Torrigiani Palace and destined it to house the *Astronomical Observatory* and the *Tribune of Galileo Galilei.* It is a unique museum in Italy because of its botanical, zoological, anatomical and mineralogical collections.

Topographical Museum of "Florence as it was". It is located near the Cathedral opposite to the Hospital of Santa Maria Nuova and has a beautiful portico by Buontalenti. The entrance to the Museum is on via S. Egidio, where at one time, was the convent of the Oblate Nuns. Its splendid rooms were restored to their original state and it contains a rich, ample photographic and pictorial documentation that allows the visitor to get an idea of the monuments and aspect of the Florence of yesterday.

Convent of Santa Maria Maddalena dei Pazzi. In the *Chapter room* of this convent (via della Colonna 9, bus N. 6) is the famous triptych frescoed by Perugino. For the visit ring at the house of the custodian at N. 7 or contact the custodian of the High School at N. 5. Here the artist painted the *Crucifixion* (1493-96), that occupies the entire wall and is divided into three arches. In the center *Christ Crucified* with *Mary Magdalen*; on the sides, *St. Bernard, the Madonna, St. John the Evangelist* and *St. Benedict* immersed in teir profound and human resignation. The chiaroscuro effects are magnificent and in the background is a wide and splendid Umbrian landscape. Farther ahead to the right, on Via Farini is the

Sinagogue. (Monumental plan N. 25), it was built by Micheli and Treves between 1872-74 (fig. 192), and is advisable to visit at sunset in order to better admire the Moorish style and decoration. For the visit contact the custodian in charge; if the gate is closed, pass through the small gate on the right.

Chiostro dello Scalzo (Via Cavour, N. 69, near Piazza San Marco next to the Buontalenti Palace, now seat of the Court of Appeals). Ring for the custodian in order to visit the graceful *"Chiostro dello Scalzo"* (seat of the Confraternity of St. John the Baptist, called "dello Scalzo" because in a procession, the cross-bearer walked barefooted). On the walls, painted in chiaro-scuro, are *Episodes in the life of St. John the Baptist* by Andrea del Sarto (1515-25), and continued by Franciabigio in the period when the artist was in Paris.

Coenaculum of the Convent of Sant'Apollonia (Via XVII Aprile, 1 - near Piazza San Marco. Monumental plan N. 6 - contact custodian). The building presently hosts the University for Foreigners and the student cafeteria. Works of restoration are in course of the Museum of Andrea del Castagno, by whom is the fresco of the *Last Supper* (1450), famous for its bold and dramatic realism.

Coenaculum of the old Convent of Foligno. By ringing the custodian of via Faenza, 42, we can admire the Refectory of the ex-Convent of the Franciscans in which there is a *Last Supper* by Perugino,

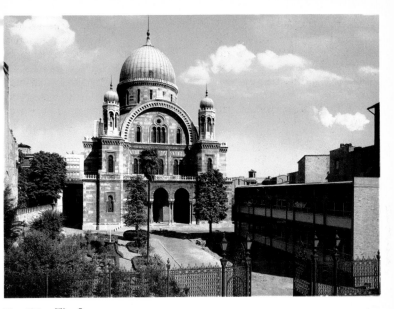

Fig. 192 - The Synagogue

brought to light in 1895 but still discussed stylistically. Leaving here and reaching via Nazionale, opposite to via dell'Ariento (animated street of the Central Market), observe the beautiful *Tabernacle with Madonna and Saints* in glazed terra-cotta by Giovanni Della Robbia (1522).

Coenaculum of San Salvi. (Belonging to the old Abbey of the Vallombrosian Monks). Located on via San Salvi N. 16 - Plan N. 42 - (Before visiting the church, contact the Direction of the Galleries in the Uffizi for information as to whether it is still closed for restorations). Among the works of Andrea del Sarto this *Last Supper* is admired for its design, color and formal rendering of *Christ* and the *Apostles,* and is considered the greatest masterpiece of this artist considered "without errors". Among other works is the fragment of the *Monument to St. Giovanni Gualberti* by Benedetto da Rovezzano and the important gallery of plaster casts of Lorenzo Bartolini. To the visitor with an automobile we suggest seeing the nearby

Stadium (plan N. 44), in the vast Campo di Marte with entrance on viale Manfredo Fanti. (If closed, ring for the custodian). It is a bold work in reinforced concrete by Pier Luigi Nervi (1932).

Pools. Now located in all outskirts of the city.

Castle of Vincigliata. As shown on the monumental map (N. 41), with one's own means we reach the Ponte a Mensola, where on the left, among the green cypresses we see the Villa "I Tatti" once owned by the American art historian Berenson who willed it to Harvard University. Continuing upwards among the picturesque hills of Fiesole and Settignano, we reach the famous Castle of Vincigliata. Although it is not possible to visit because it is private property, this excursion is particularly interesting for the pleasantness of the woods of pine and cypress trees that surround the Castle. Farther ahead, arriving at the fork for Fiesole, turning to the right, we descend to the nearby picturesque town of Settignano (plan N. 40); bus N. 7 from Piazza San Marco.

Settignano. This was the cradle of great artists like Desiderio da Settignano, the Rossellino and da Maiano brothers. After Settignano, on the right the picturesque via Rossellino, winding through a marvelous landscape of olive groves and cypresses, we arrive at the "Villa Gamberaia" belonging to Rossellino, whose famous Italian garden ispired the "Longwood Garden" in Pennsylvania. For the visit on weekdays, contact the gardener, who lives farther ahead past the arch, at the top of the hill.

Fortress Belvedere. It is located on the hill overlooking the Boboli garden (monumental plan N. 46 - fig. 193). Take bus N. 13 to the Caffè Fontana, from where, walking along the picturesque via S. Leonardo, we reach the Porta S. Giorgio on the left of which is the entrance to the Fortress (1590-95). A splendid example of a military fortress, it was built by Bernardo Buontalenti, who erected it on the bastions of the Porta San Giorgio on order of Ferdinand I Medici. Ex-military barracks, it was opportunely restored and is used for art expositions and other turist manifestations. Even if the Fortress is closed, one can always go to the vast terrace to admire the magnificent panoramic view of the city.

Fortress da Basso. Located on Viale Filippo Strozzi (monumental plan N. 48), near the Central Railway Station. Called "da Basso" (lower) because of its position. It was built following a design by Antonio Sangallo for Alessandro dei Medici (1530), when he became first Duke of Florence. It now houses a barracks and an art restoration center.

Fig. 193 - The Fortress Belvedere

Russian Orthodox Church. Located on Via Leone X, N. 8, East of the Fortress da Basso (plan N. 48). It is easily recognizable because of its small green and gilded cupolas.

Monastery of the Certosa. Built in a suggestive location at the doors of the picturesque countryside of Chianti (fig. 194). Bus N. 31 from Piazza S. Maria Novella: distance 6 km. from the city. Closed from 12 to 2:30 p.m. It was founded by Niccolò Acciaioli (1310), Grand Senescal of the King of Naples and Viceroy of Apulia. The monastery is unique in Italy because of its particular position, its architecture and the disposition of the cells. Recently, radical restorations have been made in the large halls, where numerous works of art and the celebrated frescoes by Pontormo, have been placed. The Carthusians, now reduced to a few monks, have been substituted by the Cistercians who accompany the visitors illustrating the works of art.

Florentine and Medicean Villas. If one wishes to partecipate in the organized visits held in Spring and Summer, he can consult any travel agency or his own hotel director. These sources have information about the visits and also about all the manifestations of art and folklore.

Villa or Stibbert Museum. Located North of the city in the picturesque hillside of Montughi (distance of 3 km. from the center). Bus N. 1 from via Cerretani which stops on via Vittorio Emanuele II, in front of Villa Fabbricotti, residence of Queen Victoria of England during her second trip to Florence. Farther ahead to the right is via Stibbert leading to the villa which houses the Stibbert Museum, willed to the city of Florence in 1906 by the collector Frederick Stibbert. It contains a vast collection of costumes, furniture, stuffs and is enriched by the celebrated Cavalcade, made up of 14 armed cavaliers wearing XVI cent. costumes. The visit is accompanied by the personnel of the Museum. After the tour the visitor can relax in the splendid park.

Cascine Park. Bus N. 17 (see plan N. 29). This splendid park, formerly the homestead of the Grand Ducal families, was opened to the public in the XVIII century. The ample park stretches lengthwise along the Arno up to the confluence with the Mugnone. It is very relaxing and especially suited for strolls and get togethers. Among the local festivals held here we mention the "Festa del grillo" (of the cricket), which takes place on Ascension day. There are also many sports facilities (hippodrome, tennis courts, pools).

Fig. 194 - Monastery of the Certosa

Fig. 195 - Cascine Park - Monument to an Indian Prince

In the middle of the park, on the right of the large square is the School of Forestry and Agrarian Sciences. Ahead is the small zoo and the School of Oeronatics. The park ends with the *bust* of the Indian Prince Rajarama Cuttraputi (fig. 195), who died in Florence in 1870 at 20 years of age. This small monument by Fuller is popularly called "Indiano", and commemorates the place where the young prince was cremated. Not being able to disperse the ashes in the Ganges, they were scattered at the point where the Arno meets the Mugnone.

An excursion to this park is particularly recommended as a conclusion of a visit to Florence. The vision of the numerous and incomparable works of art seen, finds a worthy cornice in the green of this magnificent park.

INDEX OF THE MAIN ARTISTS

Molenaer, Jan Meinsz (XVII sec.).
Mor, Anthony (XVI sec.).
Morales, Luis de (1500-1586).

Nattier, Jean Marc (1685-1766).
Nardo di Cione (1343-65).

Orcagna, Andrea (Andrea di Cione) (1308-68).

Palma il Vecchio (Jacopo Negretti) (1480-1528).
Paolo Uccello (Paolo di Dono) (1397-1475).
Parigi, Alfonso (XVI sec.).
Parmigianino (Francesco Mazzola) (1503-1540).
Perugino (Pietro Vannucci) (1445-1523).
Piazzetta, Giovanni Battista (1682-1754).
Pietro della Francesca (m. 1492).
Piero di Cosimo (1462-1521).
Pino, Paolo (XVI sec.).
Pollaiolo Antonio (Antonio Benci) (1433-1498).
Pollaiolo, Piero (Piero Benci) (1443-96).
Pontormo (Jacopo Carrucci) (1494-1557).

Rubens, Pierre Paul (1577-1640).
Ruysdael, Jacob van (1626-82).

Reni, Guido (1585-1642).
Rigaud, Hyacinthe (1659-1743).
Rosso Fiorentino (Giovanni Battista di Jacopo) (1494-1541).
Raffaello, Sanzio (1483-1520).
Rembrandt, Harmensz Van Rijn (1606-69).

Savoldo, Girolamo (c. 1480 - c. 1548).
Sebastiano del Piombo (Sebastiano Luciani) (1485-1547).
Signorelli, Luca (1411-1523).
Sodoma (Giovanni Antonio Bazzi) (1477-1549).
Sustermans, Justus (1597-1681).

Tintoretto, Domenico (Domenico Robusti) (1562-1637).
Tintoretto, Jacopo (Jacopo Robusti) (1518-1594).
Tura, Cosmè (1520-1595).
Tiziano (Tiziano Vecelio) (1490-1576).

Van Dyck, Anthony (1599-1641).
Vasari, Giorgio (1511-74).
Veronese (Paolo Caliari) (1528-88).
Verrocchio, Andrea del (Andrea di Cione) (1435-88).

Weyden, Roger van der (1399-1464).